SERIES EDITORS

TRACY L. PELLETT   JACK RUTHERFORD   CLAUDIA BLACKMAN

Skills, Drills & Strategies for

Strength Training

David Newberry
Kurt Kaufman
John Baker

Southern Illinois University Edwardsville

Holcomb Hathaway, Publishers
Scottsdale, Arizona 85250

Library of Congress Cataloging-in-Publication Data

Newberry, David.
    Skills, drills & strategies for strength training / David
Newberry, Kurt Kaufman, John Baker.
        p.   cm. — (The teach, coach, play series)
    Includes index.
    ISBN 1-890871-09-5
    1. Weight training. I. Kaufman, Kurt. II. Baker, John, 1939–
. III. Title. IV. Title: Skills, drills, and strategies for
strength training. V. Title: Strength training. VI. Series.
GV546.N48 2000
613.7'13—dc21   99–39948
                                                          CIP

Copyright © 2000 by Holcomb Hathaway, Publishers, Inc.

Holcomb Hathaway, Publishers
6207 North Cattle Track Road, Suite 5
Scottsdale, Arizona 85250
(480) 991-7881
www.hh-pub.com

10 9 8 7 6 5 4 3 2

ISBN 1-890871-09-5

Printed in the United States of America.

Contents

SECTION 2 Exercises 19

SECTION 3 Design 65

SECTION 4   Strategies and Special Considerations   85

SECTION 5   Glossary   105

Preface

The books in the *Teach, Coach, Play* series emphasize a systematic learning approach to sports and activities. Both visual and verbal information are presented so that you can easily understand the material and improve your performance.

Built-in learning aids help you master each skill in a step-by-step manner. Using the cues, summaries, skills, drills, and illustrations will help you build a solid foundation for safe and effective participation now and in the future.

This text is designed to illustrate correct techniques and demonstrate how to achieve optimal results. Take a few minutes to become familiar with the textbook's organization and features. Knowing what to expect and where to look for material will help you get the most out of the textbook, your practice time, and this course.

Your needs are changing, your courses are changing, your students are changing, and the demands from your administration are changing. By setting out to create a series of books that addresses many of these changes, we've created a series that:

- Provides complete, consistent coverage of each sport—the basics through skills and drills to game strategies so you can meet the needs of majors and non-majors alike.
- Includes teaching materials so that new and recently assigned instructors have the resources they need to teach the course.
- Allows you to cover exactly the sports and activities you want with the depth of coverage you want.

What's in the *Teach, Coach, Play* Series?

- Nine activities:
    Skills, Drills, & Strategies for Badminton
    Skills, Drills, & Strategies for Basketball
    Skills, Drills, & Strategies for Bowling
    Skills, Drills, & Strategies for Golf

Skills, Drills, & Strategies for Racquetball

Skills, Drills, & Strategies for Strength Training

Skills, Drills, & Strategies for Swimming

Skills, Drills, & Strategies for Tennis

Skills, Drills, & Strategies for Volleyball

■ Accompanying Instructor's Manuals

What's in the Student *Teach, Coach, Play* Textbooks?

The basic approach in all of the *Teach, Coach, Play* activity titles is to help students improve their skills and performance by building mastery from simple to complex levels.

The basic organization in each textbook is as follows:

Section 1 overviews history, organizations and publications, conditioning activities, safety, warm-up suggestions, and equipment.

Section 2 covers exercises or skills, participants, action involved, rules, facility or field, scoring, and etiquette.

Section 3 focuses on skills and drills or program design.

Section 4 addresses a broad range of strategies specifically designed to improve performance now and in the future.

Section 5 provides a convenient glossary of terms.

Supplements to Support You and Your Students

The *Teach, Coach, Play* books provide useful and practical instructional tools. Each activity is supported by its own manual. Each of these instructor's manuals includes classroom management notes, safety guidelines, teaching tips, ideas for inclusion of students with special needs, drills, lesson plans, evaluation notes, test bank, and a list of resources for you.

About the Authors

David Newberry received a Bachelor of Science degree in Sport Studies from West London Institute and a Master of Science in Education degree from Southern Illinois University Edwardsville. Currently, he is teaching at Newman College of Higher Education in London. He has worked in the broad area of fitness for the past 10 years, but his prime interest is in the sport of soccer, in which he has participated as an amateur and semi-professional player and for which he coaches in Great Britain as an FA certified coach.

Kurt Kaufman received a Bachelor of Science degree in Kinesiology from the University of Illinois and a Master of Science degree from Southern Illinois University Edwardsville. His prime interest is the field of fitness, and he is a certified strength and conditioning specialist. He has worked as a fitness director at a Nautilus Fitness/Racquet Center, as a personal trainer, and presently is strength coach for Hammer Bodies Fitness Clinic in St. Louis, Missouri. He resides in Godfrey, Illinois.

John Baker is a professor and chairperson of the Department of Kinesiology and Health Education at Southern Illinois University Edwardsville. He obtained his teacher certification in physical education at Loughborough College in England and a Master of Arts and Doctor of Philosophy from The University of Iowa. He played professional rugby in France, is an ardent tennis player and golfer, and has competed recreationally as a marathon runner. Dr. Baker's interest in and practice of weight training has been an integral part of all of these activities. He resides in Edwardsville, Illinois.

Preliminaries

After reading this section, the student will be able to do the following:

- Describe the origins of weight training and understand how it has progressed
- Understand the physical benefits associated with weight training
- Understand how weight training can increase the wellness of life
- Resolve common misconceptions regarding weight training

This section of the text begins with a brief account of the history of weight training, followed by the physical and wellness benefits of lifting, and a discussion of popular misconceptions. A number of commonly asked questions also are presented, and answers are provided. This section concludes with a list of prominent organizations that provide training courses, instructional and academic journals, and conferences for the weight training industry.

WEIGHT TRAINING: HISTORY, BENEFITS, AND MISCONCEPTIONS

History of Weight Training

The origins of weight training are not known but since the beginning of time people have exercised with weights in various forms, resulting in larger and stronger muscles. The first recorded use of weights was the ancient Greeks lifting large stones as a way of showing superior strength. Many historians believe that this was the first recording of weight training as a competitive sport. Later, in the first and second century A.D., the Greek historian Epictetus also wrote of athletes using heavy stones called **pestles** to train for competitive events. The pestle was a carved stone with a thin handle, rounded on one end, that resembled the modern day dumbbell.

The ancient Egyptian military used weight lifting, running, jumping, and mock fighting to increase strength and agility in their everyday training. Many of the civilian lower classes also used weight lifting as a means of increasing their strength, which was deemed essential for their everyday work.

The Romans participated in weight lifting contests for both men and women in the Actian Games as early as the ninth century A.D. Like the Egyptians, the Romans also used weight lifting as a way of training their military. The leaders of the

pestle *type of stone used by the Greeks in weight training that resembles the modern-day dumbbell*

1

empire encouraged soldiers to engage in the lifting of weights, running, and swimming to ready themselves for battle. Many of the Roman philosophers became interested in the wholesome effects that exercise had on people, and Galen detailed the first theories of training when he wrote of how to quantify exercise by a change in breathing habits, how exercise calmed the nerves, and of the benefits of being coached in exercise.

There is little recorded history of weight training from the time of the Roman Empire until the formation of the modern Olympic Games, in 1896, when weight lifting became part of the training regimen of athletes. From this time, scientists, athletes, and coaches have investigated the benefits associated with weight training and how to optimize performance.

The biggest changes in the style and procedures of weight training have occurred during the last 50 years. After World War II, scientists began to explore how weight training developed the body. This scientific approach enabled athletes and coaches to see the benefits that weight training possessed and the importance of training the entire body instead of only the muscles used in their performance. Before this time, coaches believed that working with weights had detrimental effects on an athlete's performance.

With the fitness boom of the 1970s, the benefits of weight training were seen for a larger population, not only to increase muscular size and strength, but as a companion of cardiovascular exercise to improve overall fitness.

Physical Benefits of Weight Training

The benefits of physical fitness can be broken down into five components: (a) cardiovascular (aerobic) endurance, (b) muscular strength and size, (c) muscular endurance, (d) flexibility and joint stability, and (e) body composition.

Cardiovascular Endurance

cardiovascular endurance
ability of the lungs, heart, and blood vessels to deliver oxygen to the body during prolonged physical activity

Cardiovascular endurance refers to the ability of the lungs, heart, and blood vessels to deliver oxygen to the body during prolonged physical activity. Activities that aid in increasing cardiovascular endurance include walking, jogging, biking, rowing, and cross-country skiing. Such activities keep the heart rate elevated for long periods of time. Cardiovascular endurance also may be improved through weight training as long as the sessions are of sufficient volume and intensity.

Muscular Strength and Size

muscular strength
amount of force a muscle can exert against a resistance in one maximal effort

One of the most noticeable physical changes associated with weight training is an increase in **muscular strength** that can be defined as the amount of force a muscle can exert against a resistance in one maximal effort. Muscular strength is associated with **hypertrophy**, which is the increase in muscle mass caused by increasing the size and number of muscle cells. Hypertrophy provides muscles with the ability to store and use more force than was previously present.

hypertrophy increase in muscle mass caused by increasing the size and number of muscle cells

Muscular Endurance

muscular endurance
ability of muscles to persist in exerting a force over a period of time

Muscular endurance refers to the ability of the muscles to exert force over a period of time. Through weight training, the muscles are able to use oxygen more efficiently for an extended duration. Since more oxygen becomes available, muscles can create force and withstand it for a longer period of time. Muscular endurance is especially important to people who participate in such athletic events as distance running, bicycling, and soccer.

Flexibility and Joint Stability

It generally is believed that weight training causes muscles to become stiff and partially immobile. Recent studies, however, have shown that with proper exercise, the **flexibility** of a muscle can be increased. Flexibility refers to the range of movement around a joint. Since tendons, which secure the muscle to the bone, run across bone joints, an increase in muscular size and strength also allows the tendons to become stronger and make the joint more stable. This helps in guarding against injuries such as a **dislocation,** in which bones become separated at a joint.

Body Composition

Body composition is a term used to describe the amount of fat and nonfat components of muscles, organs, bones, and fluids that make up the body. Body composition is usually described as the percentage of body fat weight in regard to the total amount of weight of an individual. For example, if an individual is 150 pounds of which 30 pounds is fat, the individual is said to have a body fat percentage of 20. Table 1.1 shows the average range of body fat for males and females. As stated before, as an individual becomes stronger through weight training, the muscle cells increase in size. As this happens, they will occupy a larger percentage of the body and thus cause the percentage of body fat to decrease. Body fat percentage also decreases as the body uses fat reserves for additional energy.

Two other benefits of weight training that are not directly related to the four components of physical fitness are the body's abilities to increase its metabolic rate and to increase its bone strength and density.

flexibility possible range of movement of a joint and the surrounding muscle

dislocation injury in which the bones are separated at a joint

body composition amount of fat and non-fat components that make up the body

TABLE 1.1 Body composition classification according to percent body fat.

MEN				
Age	Excellent	Good	Moderate	Overweight	Significantly Overweight
≤19	12.0	12.1–17.0	17.1–22.0	22.1–27.0	≥27.1
20–29	13.0	13.1–18.0	18.1–23.0	23.1–28.0	≥28.1
30–39	14.0	14.1–19.0	19.1–24.0	24.1–29.0	≥29.1
40–49	15.0	15.1–20.0	20.1–25.0	25.1–30.0	≥30.1
≥50	16.0	16.1–21.0	21.1–26.0	26.1–31.0	≥31.1

WOMEN				
Age	Excellent	Good	Moderate	Overweight	Significantly Overweight
≤19	17.0	17.1–22.0	22.1–27.0	27.1–32.0	≥32.1
20–29	18.0	18.1–23.0	23.1–28.0	28.1–33.0	≥33.1
30–39	19.0	19.1–24.0	24.1–29.0	29.1–34.0	≥34.1
40–49	20.0	20.1–25.0	25.1–30.0	30.1–35.0	≥35.1
≥50	21.0	21.1–26.0	26.1–31.0	31.1–36.0	≥36.1

Metabolic Rate

nutrients *compounds used by the body to provide energy and to aid in growth and repair*

The food we eat is made up of **nutrients** that are responsible for providing the energy needed by the body, as well as helping with its growth and repair. Nutrients are classified as carbohydrates, fat, protein, vitamins, minerals, or water. Of these, the first three are the primary fuels that provide the body with its energy. Excess energy intake is stored in the form of fat, no matter which nutrient provides the excess.

metabolism *rate at which the body uses energy*

The rate at which the body uses energy is referred to as its **metabolism**. This is greatly affected by weight training since muscles are constantly in use, and the demand for energy is great. With an increase in the size of muscle cells as a result of weight training, the body needs more energy to accomplish its everyday activities. This increased need for energy speeds up the body's metabolism to produce energy faster and more efficiently and also to allow the body to use the stored fat.

Bone Strength and Density

bone strength *amount of force that bones are able to withstand*

bone mineral density *amount of mineral deposited in a given area of bone*

osteoporosis *loss in bone mineral density and subsequent weakening of bone*

The stress placed on bones during weight training causes them to become stronger. Since weight training applies more force than the body is accustomed to, it must adapt by making the bones stronger and able to withstand a greater amount of force. **Bone Strength** is obtained primarily through an increase in **bone mineral density,** which refers to the amount of mineral deposited in a given area of bone. The greater the density of mineral in the bone, the more stress it is able to withstand. Conversely, loss in bone mineral density weakens the bone, resulting in a condition called **osteoporosis**.

Wellness Benefits of Weight Training

wellness *constant and deliberate effort to stay healthy and achieve the highest potential for well-being*

Besides the physical well-being associated with weight training, the entire **wellness** of an individual will benefit from a structured program. Wellness is defined as the constant and deliberate effort to stay healthy and achieve the highest potential for well-being. As well as physical fitness, the mental, social, and emotional aspects of life are included in this total wellness. Weight training also will aid in enhancing these aspects of an individual's well-being.

A proper weight training program requires a person to understand how the body functions, responds, and adapts to exercise. Logical planning, self-discipline, self-analysis, and problem-solving skills are required to endure a safe and effective weight training program. This type of program also provides the opportunity to develop positive social qualities. Sharing, caring, encouraging, and helping behaviors are developed while training in a group environment. Unlike other sporting events, weight training allows each participant to be a winner and provides results that are both positive and noticeable. Weight training also can be seen as a means of bringing a group of people together who communicate on a common topic. Research has shown that muscular tension will decrease following a single bout of exercise, thus releasing physical and mental stress, which helps increase a person's self-esteem, physical self-image, overall health, and attitude.

Common Misconceptions Concerning Weight Training

The inception of weight training as a useful tool has generated many misconceptions largely because of "experts" who unwillingly give poor advice to people beginning a weight training program. Before seeking assistance with a weight training program, participants should check the background of instructors to make sure that they are qualified to provide safe and knowledgeable instruction.

In addition, several national and international organizations offer certification programs to provide people with the skills needed to design a weight training program. Many people who are reluctant to begin a weight training program ask one or more of the following questions:

If I stop weight training will my muscle turn to fat? No. muscle and fat tissue are entirely different compounds within the body. Muscle cannot become fat nor fat become muscle. As the body becomes stronger through a weight training program, muscles adapt by becoming large and dense. At the same time, much of the energy needed to maintain the increased amount of muscle comes from burning fat. When a person stops a weight training program, muscles and fat will adapt in the opposite manner. Since less demand is placed on the muscle, the muscle cells become smaller and less dense and fat cells are not needed to provide excess energy.

Will weight training cause a woman to become bulky like a man? No. It is the role of hormones rather than weight training that gives people their masculine and feminine characteristics. Males have approximately 6 to 10 times more testosterone than females, and it is the higher levels of this hormone that contribute to secondary male characteristics. In most cases, women who train with weights will develop stronger and firmer muscles resulting in greater muscle tone.

Will weight training damage my joints? No. When weight training is performed in a correct manner, the strength and mobility of the joints are increased.

Will weight training make me look like a bodybuilder? No. While weight training does have the potential of creating very large and shapely muscles, it does not turn everyone into a massive bodybuilder. The potential to increase muscle size is primarily related to genetic factors. By performing proper exercises with correct weight and the right number of sets and repetitions, weight training allows a person to increase or decrease overall body size to suit specific goals.

How do I know if I am too young or too old to start a weight training program? Weight training is designed to benefit people of all ages. Prior to beginning any exercise program, however, it is best to consult a physician or talk with a knowledgeable instructor who will design a program to suit your specific needs. Weight training also can be beneficial for young adolescents when performed in a safe and supervised manner, but again, it is best to consult a qualified physician to determine a level of activity that can be safely undertaken.

Types of Weight Training

Everyone who trains with weights can be considered a weight trainer. However, as stated earlier, weight training can benefit people in several ways. The following categories will aid in understanding how similar activity causes a variety of changes in different individuals.

Olympic Lifting

Olympic weight lifting is a competitive sport that requires the participants to lift weights in a very powerful manner. The two types of Olympic lifts are the *clean and jerk* and the *snatch*. The clean and jerk lift requires the participant to bring a weighted bar from the floor to the upper chest and shoulders. From this position, the lifter thrusts the bar overhead for a straight-armed finish. The snatch requires the lifter to bring the weighted bar from the floor to an overhead position in one continuous movement.

Power Lifting

Power lifting is another competitive sport that requires participants to perform the bench press, squat, and dead lift. The individual who lifts the most combined amount of weight is declared the winner.

Bodybuilding

Bodybuilders participate in a competition where each person is judged on their muscular size and physique. Bodybuilders use weight training to maximize the size and shape of each muscle.

Circuit Training

Circuit training is normally performed on a series of weight machines that emphasize individual body parts. In circuit training, the individual often moves as quickly as possible from one exercise to the other, limiting the time of rest in-between. While circuit training minimizes the total amount of training time, it requires the participant to exert a large amount of energy in a short period of time.

Organizations

Several organizations offer literature and seminars for people interested in weight training and fitness. A number of these provide various levels of certification for instructors to assure the general population that these instructors are qualified to give knowledgeable and proper advice and instruction. It is important, therefore, to find out the qualifications of fitness professionals before accepting their services. Following is a list of some of these organizations:

American Alliance for Health, Physical Education, Recreation, and Dance (AAHPERD)
1900 Association Dr.
Reston, VA 22091
www.aahperd.org

American College of Sports Medicine (ACSM)
P.O. Box 1440
Indianapolis, In 46206-1440
www.acsm.org

International Dance-Exercise Association (IDEA)
2431 Morena Blvd., Suite 2-D
San Diego, CA 92110
www.ideafit.com

National Academy of Sports Medicine (NASM)
2434 N. Greenview
Chicago, IL 60614

National Strength and Conditioning Association (NSCA)
1955 N. Union Blvd.
Colorado Springs, CO 80909
719-632-6722
www.nsca-lift.org

United States Weightlifting Federation (USWF)
One Olympic Plaza
Colorado Springs, CO 80909
719-578-4508
www.usaw.org

YMCA of the USA
101 N. Wacker Dr.
Chicago, IL 60606

Summary

It has been widely documented that during the ancient Greek and Roman civilizations, athletes, soldiers, and everyday citizens used weights as a means of improving both physical fitness and performance. After World War II, scientists performed experiments to determine how the body responds to weight training. As positive results were found, athletes and coaches began to use weight training as a means of enhancing performance.

Weight training can lead to many physical adaptations of the body. Muscles increase their strength, endurance, and overall size, and bones also begin to strengthen, thereby delaying the onset of osteoporosis. Flexibility and joint stability increase with weight training. The body also experiences mental adaptations that enhance well-being, spiritual life, and emotional status, leading to an overall increase in a person's wellness. While many people have fears about beginning weight training, a properly designed program can result in positive outcomes. However, before beginning a program, participants should obtain proper instruction from trained personnel. Many organizations are available to the public that offer certification to people interested in the fitness field, as well as educational resources.

ANATOMY AND PHYSIOLOGY OF WEIGHT TRAINING

After reading this section, the student will be able to do the following:

- Understand the physical and functional differences between skeletal, cardiac, and smooth muscles
- Have a general knowledge of the components that make up skeletal muscles
- Know how the different energy systems are used by the body during exercise
- Understand the general mechanics of how a skeletal muscle contraction occurs as well as the different types of contractions that may occur
- Differentiate between muscle fiber types
- Understand how muscles work together to produce force and movement
- Understand the general theories regarding the cause of muscle soreness

This section of the text describes the different types of muscles in the body, their structure, how they obtain energy, the mechanics of a contraction, the different types of contraction, and how movement is generated. In addition, different types of muscle fibers are presented, along with a description of how muscle soreness is produced.

Types of Muscles

The body comprises over 400 muscles, which coordinate their contractions to stabilize it and produce smooth movement (see figure 1.1). With effective training, the muscles can become stronger, thus allowing greater force output and better endurance.

The three types of muscles found in the body are cardiac, smooth, and skeletal. As its name implies, **cardiac muscle** is associated with the heart. It differs from the other types of muscle in that its fibers are interwoven to permit the wavelike impulses of the nervous system. At rest, cardiac muscle is able to contract at a constant pace of approximately 70 times per minute, with the ability to increase its rate during exertion. **Smooth muscle** is commonly associated with our other organs and is able to contract without conscious effort. For example, the digestive system is lined with smooth muscles, which contract involuntarily to move food from the esophagus to the stomach and to the intestines.

cardiac muscle muscle that is associated with the heart

smooth muscle muscle associated with the internal organs; smooth muscle is able to contract

Figure 1.1

Human musculature: anterior and posterior views.

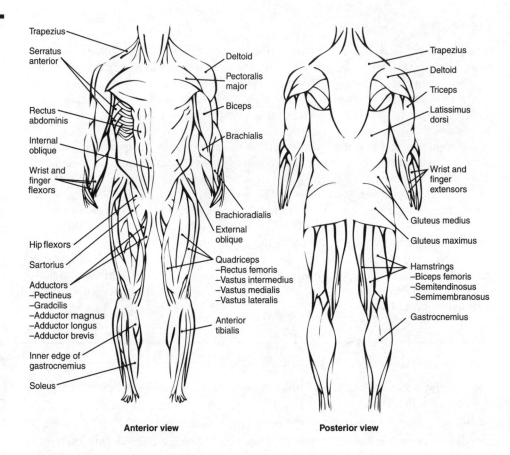

Trapezius
Serratus anterior
Deltoid
Pectoralis major
Biceps
Brachialis
Rectus abdominis
Internal oblique
Wrist and finger flexors
Brachioradialis
External oblique
Hip flexors
Sartorius
Quadriceps
–Rectus femoris
–Vastus intermedius
–Vastus medialis
–Vastus lateralis
Adductors
–Pectineus
–Gradcilis
–Adductor magnus
–Adductor longus
–Adductor brevis
Anterior tibialis
Inner edge of gastrocnemius
Soleus

Trapezius
Deltoid
Triceps
Latissimus dorsi
Wrist and finger extensors
Gluteus medius
Gluteus maximus
Hamstrings
–Biceps femoris
–Semitendinosus
–Semimembranosus
Gastrocnemius

Anterior view   **Posterior view**

skeletal muscle *muscles that are responsible for the movements of the body and support of the skeletal system*

fasciculi *bundles of muscle fibers*

endomysium *outermost structure of the muscle*

myofibrils *make up the muscle fiber and are the site of muscular contraction*

actin *fine protein thread of the muscle that is important for muscular contraction*

myosin *fine protein thread of the muscle that is important for muscular contraction*

adenosine triphosphate (ATP) *energy-rich compound that provides the energy used by the body*

The majority of our muscles fall into the **skeletal muscle** category. These are responsible for the movements of the body and give support to our skeletal system. Since they are the primary type of muscles in the body and are responsible for human movement, the focus of this section will be on the structure and function of these muscles.

Skeletal Muscle Structure

When examining a single skeletal muscle, one finds that it is comprised of several bundles of fibers called **fasciculi**. The outermost connective tissue of the muscle is called the **endomysium**, which binds together each individual fiber to form larger bundles. These muscle fibers are long and cylindrical and contain many **myofibrils**, which allow muscular contraction to take place (see figure 1.2). Each myofibril contains two types of protein threads called **actin** and **myosin**, which play an important role in the muscle contraction process.

Energy Systems

For muscles to contract and produce movement, the body supplies them with energy from a breakdown of foods that we eat. The energy in the food is not directly used by the muscle cells but, instead, is transferred through a succession of chemical reactions to produce an energy-rich compound called **adenosine triphosphate (ATP)**. It is the breakdown of the ATP that provides the energy used not only by the muscles, but by all the systems of the body. Since the body is constantly using energy and not much ATP is stored, it must be constantly resynthe-

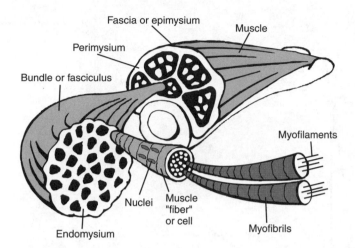

Figure 1.2
Structure of a muscle.

sized to sustain the levels needed by the body. This can be achieved through three energy systems: the ATP-PC system, the anaerobic (lactic acid) system, and the aerobic system.

ATP-CP System

The muscles are able to store small mounts of ATP and a chemical called **creatine phosphate** (**CP**), which is important in the resynthesis of ATP. These stores, called **phosphagens**, can be used by the body in explosive physical activities such as sprinting, jumping, and lifting for up to 10 seconds. Once these stores are depleted, the muscles must either rest to restore their levels of ATP and CP or obtain additional ATP from the other systems.

creatine phosphate (CP) chemical important in the resynthesis of ATP

phosphagens storage form of ATP and creatine phosphate

Anaerobic (Lactic Acid) System

When activity lasts beyond 10 seconds but less than 3 minutes, the body is able to obtain ATP through the chemical breakdown of a sugar called **glucose** and its storage form, **glycogen**. This process is **anaerobic** because no oxygen is needed for the glucose to be converted into ATP. One side effect that is associated with this process, however, is the formation of **lactic acid**. Since the body is only able to supply ATP through this process for 3 minutes, the muscles, again, must rest or find other means of producing ATP.

glucose sugar stored in the body that releases energy used to form ATP

glycogen storage form of glucose

anaerobic without oxygen

lactic acid chemical formed during the breakdown of glucose to ATP when oxygen is not present

Aerobic System

When the body is able to convert glucose to ATP in the presence of oxygen, it is referred to as an **aerobic** system. Since oxygen is present, the formation of lactic acid is minimal and activity is able to continue for long periods of time. The body produces its energy through the aerobic system for any activity that lasts longer than 3 minutes. Figure 1.3 shows the contributions made by each of the energy systems during physical activity.

aerobic in the presence of oxygen

Muscular Contraction

In a relaxed state, the heads of the thin filament myosin lie in close proximity to thick filaments of actin (see figure 1.4A) but are unable to bind with them because the connecting sites are blocked by a protein called **tropomyosin**. However, when

tropomyosin protein that inhibits muscular contraction

Figure 1.3
Contributions of the three energy systems during physical activity.

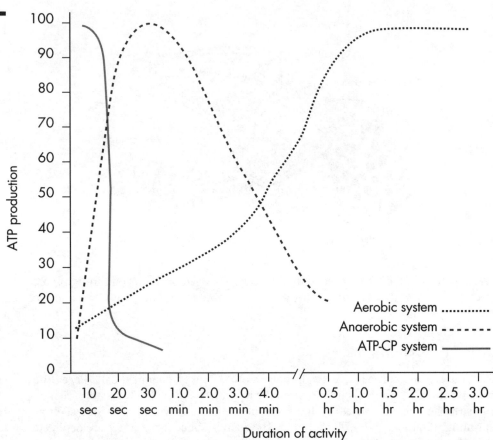

troponin protein that pulls away tropomyosin; allows muscular contraction to occur

sliding filament theory common theory regarding muscular contraction

isotonic contraction performed by maintaining a constant force

isokinetic contraction performed at a constant speed

isometric muscular contraction during which the length of the muscle remains unchanged

concentric contraction in which the muscle shortens

eccentric contraction in which the muscle exerts force as it lengthens

a nerve impulse is sent to the muscle, another protein, **troponin**, pulls the tropomyosin away from the actin (see figure 1.4B) so that the myosin heads are able to bind with the actin filaments and pull them together (see figure 1.4C). The myosin then will detach from the binding site and attach to another site to continue to pull the actin together (see figure 1.4D). This process continues as long as the muscle receives a stimulus from the nervous system and ATP is broken down to release energy.

Once the nervous impulses stop, the tropomyosin again will block the binding sights to inhibit the myosin from connecting with the actin. When the actin and myosin are back to their normal positions, the muscle is said to be in the relaxed state. This theory of how the muscle contracts and relaxes is referred to as the **sliding filament theory.**

Muscle contractions can be placed into one of three categories: **isotonic, isokinetic,** or **isometric**. Isotonic contractions, which are common during weight training, occur when the shortening of the muscle fibers produces a constant force throughout the range of motion. An isokinetic contraction refers to a constant contracting of muscle fibers regardless of the forces produced. An isometric contraction is one on which minimal fiber shortening produces a force without any range of motion.

Isotonic and isokinetic contractions are often referred to as **concentric** and **eccentric** dynamic contractions. A concentric contraction refers to the shortening of the muscle as it contracts. An example of this would be the upward phase of a bicep curl. Eccentric contractions occur when a muscle exerts force as it lengthens. It is often confusing to think of a muscle contracting as it lengthens, but an example of such is the downward phase of a bicep curl. The biceps must resist the downward force of gravity to prevent the weight and arm from falling too quickly.

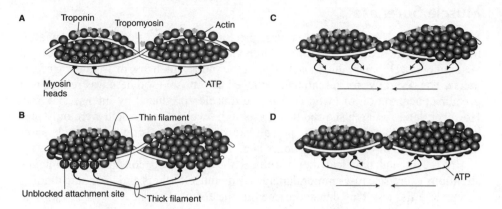

Figure 1.4
The process of muscular contraction.

Muscle Fibers

The body is thought to be made up of two different types of muscle fibers: **Type I (slow-twitch)** and **Type II (fast-twitch)**. As their names imply, the fiber types are categorized by how fast they can contract. Even though Type I fibers are called "slow-twitch," they contract fast enough for practically any physical activity. The majority of muscle fibers fall into the slow-twitch category. Slow-twitch fibers are those used for endurance. They do not produce as much force as fast-twitch fibers, but they are able to produce force over a longer period of time. Slow-twitch fibers are characterized by their great oxidative capability due to the large number of **mitochondria** located in the muscle fibers. The mitochondrion is often called the powerhouse of the cell because it converts fats, carbohydrates, and proteins into energy (ATP).

As their name suggests, fast-twitch fibers are capable of a fast contraction and, therefore, produce greater force than slow-twitch fibers. They are involved in short-term activities such as sprinting and weight lifting. The fast-twitch fibers are not able to use oxygen in the contractile process, which leads to an early fatigue and deactivation of the fibers. There are actually two types of fast-twitch fibers: Type IIa and IIb. Type IIa can be thought of as intermediate fibers that are able to contract at a fairly rapid speed and contain a small amount of mitochondria for oxygen use. Type IIb fibers can be thought of as the true fast-twitch as they are able to contract at the fastest speeds and do not have any oxidative capacities.

Type I (slow-twitch fiber) muscle fiber that is able to produce a small amount of force over a long period of time, characterized by utilizing oxygen when contracting

Type II (fast-twitch fiber) muscle fiber that is able to produce a large, rapid force

mitochondria structures in the cell where ATP is produced for energy

Muscular Force and Movement

We have examined the makeup of the muscle, the actions each fiber takes to produce a contraction, and the different types of contraction that can occur. We now turn our attention to how the muscles produce force and cause movement. There are over 200 skeletal muscles of different size, shape, and function in the body. These muscles work together in three different ways to produce force resulting in coordinated body movement.

The **agonists** or *prime movers* are the muscles that are primarily responsible for movement. In the biceps curl, for example, the biceps are the agonists. The **antagonists** are muscles that oppose the prime movers. During this type of curl, the triceps act as antagonists. **Synergists** are muscles that aid the prime movers in performing the movement. The brachioradialis acts as a synergist in this example. A smooth coordinated biceps curl requires the shortening of the prime mover (biceps) and the synergist (brachioradialis) and the relaxation of the antagonist (triceps).

agonists muscles that are primarily responsible for movement

antagonists muscles that oppose the movement of the agonists

synergists muscles that aid the agonists in performing movement

Muscle Soreness

Many individuals beginning an exercise program experience soreness the day after they have exercised. Even well-conditioned people who have trained for several years may develop pain due to a change in the mode, intensity, or frequency of exercise. For several years, researchers believed this muscle soreness was related to a greater concentration of lactic acid in the muscles produced by intense exercise. However, later research showed that these high levels of lactic acid were only present for 15 to 30 minutes after a person had stopped exercising, and muscle soreness did not occur until 24 to 48 hours later.

A recent and practical theory refutes the lactic acid concept and contends strenuous exercise causes minor damage to the muscle fibers and their surrounding connective tissues. This damage comes in the form of small tears in the muscle fibers causing a leakage of chemicals into the spaces surrounding them. These chemicals either directly stimulate nerves to sense pain or cause increases in swelling that lead to increased pressure on the nerves, causing them to sense pain.

Summary

A muscle is a complex organ containing several layers of tissue that are important for contraction to occur. When several muscles are able to coordinate their contractions over a period of time, the body is able to move in a smooth pattern. Movement occurs as isotonic (same force), isokinetic (same speed), or isometric (same movement) contractions. Muscle fibers are classified by the type of contraction they produce. Type I or slow-twitch fibers are able to withstand small amounts of stress over a long period and are those used in endurance activities. Type II or fast-twitch fibers are able to produce a large force for a short period of time and are used in quick explosive movements. A primary group of muscles called agonists, which oppose antagonists, are responsible for muscular contraction and subsequent movement. Synergist muscles aid the agonist in movement but are not responsible for the gross movement. Recent research has shown that the primary cause of muscle soreness comes from small tears in the muscle fibers. These cause a leakage of chemicals into the space surrounding the fibers and either directly stimulate the nerves to sense pain or increase the amount of swelling, resulting in pain.

EQUIPMENT AND SAFETY

After reading this section, the student will be able to do the following:

- Understand the importance of receiving medical clearance from a physician before participating in a weight training program
- Recognize the proper attire for weight training
- Identify the equipment including safety devices used in weight training
- Understand the importance and proper procedures of spotting

This section of the text provides a brief account of the equipment used during weight training, including personal clothing; free weights; machines; and safety devices, including belts, gloves, chalk, and straps. Important safety issues are presented, such as spotting, supervision, and equipment maintenance.

Medical Clearance

Each participant should have a complete examination by a physician before beginning a weight training program. This is even more critical for people who have not participated in any physical activity for a period of 6 months or longer. A medical examination screens participants for health risks such as cardiovascular disease, elevated blood pressure, elevated cholesterol, and muscle and joint problems that may inhibit them from proper physical training.

Clothing

Proper attire is important when beginning a weight training program. Most individuals select clothing that is comfortable and allows freedom of movement during all exercises. Footwear is extremely important when performing any physical activity, and this is especially true for weight training. Heavy canvas or leather shoes that cover the entire foot should be worn, as the weight room is full of items that may be accidentally kicked, dropped, or stepped on. In a warm climate or in a gymnasium, most weight training participants wear shorts and either a T-shirt or tank top. When the training climate is colder, a cotton sweat suit is often worn over shorts and shirt. Participants may want to inquire about specific dress requirements at a training location before beginning a program, as public and private facilities often have guidelines regarding the proper attire to wear in the weight room.

Safety Devices

Many people who engage in a weight training program use mechanical aids and safety devices such as weight belts, chalk, gloves, and lifting straps. While these devices may be useful in weight training, several of them often are misused and can actually cause an injury.

Weight belts are wide, thick leather belts used to stabilize and protect the lower back. These belts are beneficial safety devices when heavy weights are used for such exercises as squats, cleans, snatches, and overhead lifts. The weight belt should fit snugly around the lifter's waist with the buckle of the belt sitting just below the navel. Many individuals wear the weight belt for every exercise without regard to the amount of weight being used or the muscle group being trained. This inappropriate use of the weight belt may limit an individual from strengthening the musculature of the lower back and abdomen.

Weight lifting gloves and **chalk** often are used to improve a person's grip on the weights. Lifting gloves are usually made of soft leather, cover the palm of the hands, and fit snugly without limiting the range of motion of either the fingers or the wrist. Chalk often is used to improve the grip on the bar by absorbing perspiration on the hands and that which has transferred to the bar. Chalk should be used only in designated areas. Many gymnasiums prohibit its use due to the fine white residue that deposits itself on both the equipment and the floor.

Lifting straps are made of either durable canvas or leather and aid a lifter in maintaining proper grip and control of the bar. The strap is approximately 1 to 1 1/2 inches in width with a loop at one end. The loop is placed over the wrist and the rest of the strap is wrapped around the bar with the end of the loop grasped in the palm. Lifting straps are usually used with a heavy weight on pull-type exercises such as dead lifts, pulldowns, and rows.

weight belts wide, thick leather belts that are used to stabilize and protect the lower back

weight lifting gloves soft leather gloves that cover the palm of the hand and are used to improve the grip during weight training

chalk powder or block form of calcium carbonate that improves the grip by absorbing perspiration

lifting straps canvas or leather straps that assist a lifter in maintaining a proper grip and control of the bar

Weight Machines

Weight training offers an individual an array of equipment and exercises that can be performed for all major muscle groups. Machines range from simple elastic straps and bands to extremely complex and technical resistance machines. Each type of machine is designed to produce different results and requires varying amounts of skill.

weight machines equipment that restricts movement to ensure correct technique and safety. Weights are stacked and the resistance is altered by moving a pin that supports the weights

Several "universal" **weight machines** are available that use a stack of weights or other means to produce resistance to a movement. The machines tend to be safer and easier to use than other types of equipment. They are designed specifically to exercise single body parts and are arranged to provide a whole-body weight training routine. These machines are an advantage when the lifter is trying to isolate muscle groups that are difficult to resist with free weights. For example, a weight machine can be used to train the adductors (inner thigh) and abductors (outer thigh) of the upper leg. Also, these machines save time in selecting and changing the amount of resistance. Finally, weight machines reduce the likelihood of injury as a result of dropping or being trapped by weights. For added safety, therefore, individuals who are training alone should use weight machines. Proper setup and instruction can be obtained from a qualified individual before using any weight machine. Resistance weight machines are marketed by a large number of companies, such as Nautilus, Universal, Life Fitness, Badger, Cybex, and Paramount.

Free Weights

free weights dumbbells, barbells, and weighted plates used in weight training

Dumbbells, barbells, and weighted plates are commonly referred to as **free weights.** Free weights generally are less expensive than weight machines, take up less room, and can be used to work specific muscles. However, free weights require more coordination and expertise than weight machines. A proper weight training program normally will implement a combination of both weight machines and free weight exercises. Individuals should contact an instructor, coach, or strength and conditioning specialist before beginning any type of weight training.

Spotting and Supervision

One of the most beneficial assets for a person beginning a weight training program is a good training partner who will help spot hazardous situations, load and unload weights, assist in safe movement of the weights, and offer encouragement and motivation. This training partner is perhaps most important during the **spotting** of an exercise. Spotting refers to positioning oneself to assist a person who may be unable to safely accomplish an exercise. Two of the most important factors in effective spotting techniques are good communication and alertness. Before the exercise, lifters and spotters should talk briefly about the procedures that must take place in the event the lifters are unable to complete a lift under their own power. It is essential for the spotter to know the lift being performed, the number of repetitions being performed, and the amount of weight being used. This communication takes only a brief moment before the lift and significantly decreases the risk of injury. The spotter also must be alert if the lifter begins to have difficulty completing the exercise. To prevent injury, the spotter should offer assistance as soon as the lift stops moving in a positive direction. Even a slight pause on behalf of the spotter could have dangerous consequences for both the lifter and the spotter.

spotting assisting a person in safely accomplishing an exercise

There are differing opinions as to where pressure should be applied while spotting a dumbbell exercise. Many people suggested spotters should place their hands on the elbows or upper arms of the lifter to assist the movement. However, this position may be unsafe for the lifter. It is better to place the hands as close to the dumbbells as possible or to spot the dumbbell itself, which will offer improved balance and a more secure grip on the weights. The arrows in figures 1.5a and 1.5b show the incorrect and correct placement of the hands when spotting a dumbbell exercise. Table 1.2 lists some general guidelines for spotters.

Figures 1.6, 1.7, and 1.8 show the proper form for spotting a lifter for a series of exercises.

a

b

Figure 1.5

(a) Arrows indicate the incorrect hand placement for dumbbell fly spotting.

(b) Arrows indicate the spotter's hand placement for correct spotting for the dumbbell fly.

TABLE 1.2	General guidelines for spotters.

Be sure you are strong enough to help with the weight being attempted. If not, tell the lifter and try to find more help.

Be sure you know how the lifter expects to be spotted. If you are unsure, ask the lifter before he/she begins.

Be sure you know what signs and signals the lifter will use to communicate during the lift. Know what words and gestures the lifter will use to let you know what to do.

Stay alert. Give your full attention to spotting the lift. Keep your complete attention and concentration on the lifter.

Do not touch the bar during the exercise if the lifter can complete the lift without your help. By doing so, you may decrease the overload stimulus the lifter needs to make the desired gains.

Check the bar before the lift for balanced loading and secure collars.

Move weights and any other debris near your feet that might cause you to trip or lose balance.

Stay in a proper spotting position throughout the lift so you are ready at any moment.

Do not jerk the bar away from the lifter or throw it off balance. Gently provide the amount of help needed to complete the lift.

Be a responsible spotter! The lifter is depending on you to do the right job.

Adapted from Hesson (1995).

Figure 1.6
Spotting position for the
bench press.

Figure 1.7
Spotting positions for the
lying triceps extension.

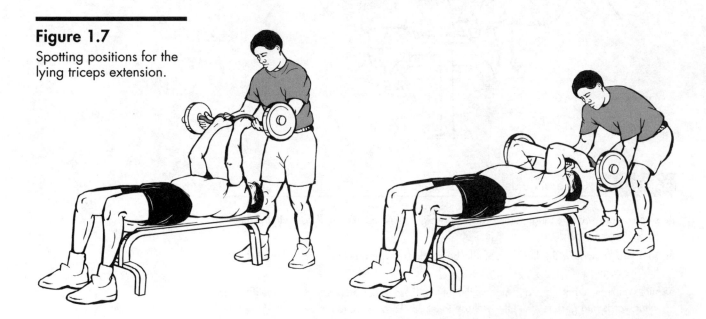

Repair and Maintenance of Equipment

Weight machines and equipment must be properly maintained. It is important to inspect any machine before using it to be certain that it is in safe working order. All bolts should be secure, ropes and pulleys should not show signs of excessive wear or fraying, and guide rods should be smooth and properly lubricated. If, upon inspection, something seems to be wrong with the machine, it should not be used. Most gymnasiums have a daily, weekly, and monthly maintenance schedule, so the weight room instructor or supervisor should be contacted if any equipment is in need of attention. If many people are using the same machines, it is courteous to carry a towel to wipe any perspiration off the machine after use.

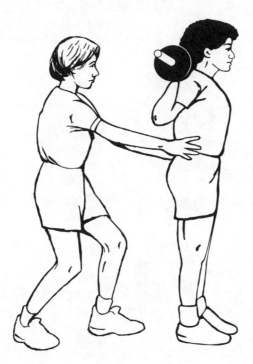

Figure 1.8
Spotting position for the lunge.

Weight training can be one of the best physical activities of overall health when the proper safety precautions are applied. As with any exercise program, medical clearance should be obtained prior to beginning a weight training program.

It is important to select clothing that is comfortable and allows freedom of movement during all exercises. Inquire about any specific dress requirements where you train since certain facilities may have specific guidelines concerning proper attire.

Many people find it advantageous to use safety devices such as weight belts, gloves chalk, or lifting straps when they train. However, these items often are overused or misused, which can result in injury or inhibit muscles from being properly strengthened. Weight training can be performed on an array of equipment ranging from simple and inexpensive elastic straps to large and expensive weight machines. Base the style of machine used upon your goals and level of expertise.

Spotting refers to positioning oneself to assist a person who is unable to safely accomplish an exercise. A good training partner should not only provide spotting, but also help in loading and unloading weights, offer encouragement and motivation, and be able to spot hazardous situations.

The repair and maintenance of weight training equipment is very important. The lifter should inspect the equipment before use to ensure it is in safe working order. Always seek professional assistance when you find a machine in an unsafe condition. Never attempt to repair the problem yourself.

SUMMARY

Exercises

After reading this section the student will be able to do the following:

- Describe the importance of the warm-up, stretching, and cooldown phases of an exercise program
- Perform warm-up, stretching, and cooldown exercises
- Understand the differences between a general and specific warm-up
- Identify the factors that affect muscle flexibility
- Discuss and perform different types of stretching techniques
- Understand the term *proprioceptive neuromuscular facilitation*

This section of the text provides a discussion of the importance of warming up and stretching prior to and cooling down and stretching after weight lifting. The benefits of a warm-up and a description of the physical adaptations occurring from an increase in activity are presented. The general and specific components of a warm-up are described and suggestions are provided for the intensity and duration of each. The benefits of stretching are highlighted, with particular reference to the development of flexibility. Examples of four different types of stretching techniques (active, static, ballistic, and passive) are described and illustrated, with one popular passive stretching technique, proprioceptive neuromuscular facilitation (PNF), discussed in detail. Descriptions and illustrations of several PNF techniques are provided for different muscles. This section concludes by outlining the benefits of cooling down after weight training.

Warm-up

Before starting a weight training program, participants should prepare muscles and their supporting structures for the stress and strain that the resistance will exert on them. All workout sessions should begin with a warm-up of approximately 10 minutes, followed by an all-round body stretching routine.

Fluency of movement from a resting condition is achieved through a gradual increase in physical activity, which produces numerous effects on bodily functions, including (a) an elevation in heart rate, required to increase the blood flow to the lungs and the working muscles; (b) an increase in blood flow, required to carry oxygen from the lungs to the working muscles; (c) an increase in the internal muscle temperature, required for efficient muscular contraction and sustained release of oxygen at the muscle tissue; (d) an increase in the release of lubricating fluid around the skeletal joints, required for fluency of movement; and (e) an improvement in bodily coordination, resulting from an increase in nerve impulse transmission at a higher temperature. A correctly performed warm-up, which can be subdivided into general and specific components, reduces the likelihood of muscle injury.

General Warm-up

general warm-up transition from rest to light exercise, consisting of any exercise that involves movement of large muscle groups

The **general warm-up** component is the transition from rest to light exercise and consists of any exercise that involves the movement of large muscle groups, such as the quadriceps, hamstrings, and pectorals. An example of a general warm-up exercise is the combination of walking with a swinging motion of the arms. This action utilizes the major muscle groups of the legs and upper body.

It is important that the general warm-up component commences at a low intensity and gradually increases. Too fast a rate, or too many wrenching movements, could result in the type of injuries that the warm-up is designed to prevent. The duration of the warm-up depends on the individual's functional responses to the exercise, the external temperature, the type of exercise being performed, and the intensity of the warm-up. An example of a correct 10-minute warm-up would be to walk at a slow pace for 2 minutes, increase the intensity to a brisk walk for 3 minutes, and then further increase the pace to a jogging speed for the final 5 minutes. Other methods of warm-up include cycling, low impact aerobics, stepping (using step machine or stepping onto a box), swimming, or using a rowing machine.

Specific Warm-up

Once the general component has been completed, the body must prepare for the specific movements of the training program. An example of a *specific warm-up* is a biceps curl with light resistance to prepare the biceps (muscles in the front of the upper arm) for a concentrated workout. This specific warm-up prepares the biceps muscles for the progression to heavier weights. Lifting heavy weights immediately following the general warm-up increases the risk of muscular injury.

When determining the intensity of the specific warm-up component for weight training, it is important to consider the strength of the muscle group and the range of movement with which the joint and surrounding structures will be required to conform. Not only is it imperative to choose the correct weight, but also to choose the correct exercise. If, for example, it is the intention of the exerciser to work the pectoral muscles (chest) using a dumbbell chest fly exercise, then it would not be suitable to use a bench press exercise as a warm-up. Performed correctly, dumbbell chest flies work the pectorals through a full *range of motion (ROM)* and utilize a larger muscle surface area than a bench press exercise. Thus, it is advisable to select a warm-up exercise that is similar to the main exercise.

repetitions number of times an exercise movement is repeated consecutively

The difference between the warm-up and the main exercise is that a lower intensity/weight is employed for the warm-up. The weight should be set at a level that allows completion of 15 to 20 **repetitions** of the movement (i.e., main exercise = biceps curl, warm-up = 15–20 biceps curl repetitions at 2–5 lbs).

Stretching

Once the warm-up is compete, it is necessary to stretch the muscles and connective tissue. Stretching is an extension of the warm-up and is as important in the preparation for the main exercise as jogging, cycling, or stepping. Failure to stretch diminishes the effectiveness of the warm-up. To stretch the muscle effectively, the stretching routine should be performed when the muscles are warm. Stretching a muscle that is in a resting state is like pulling a rubber band that has been in the freezer—one or two pulls and the band will snap. Similar to the rubber band, a muscle that is warm will stretch to a much greater length and will be less likely to tear.

There are a number of other important reasons to stretch. A regular and correctly performed stretching routine will improve the flexibility of the muscles, allowing the joint to move through a greater range of motion. Regularly stretched muscles are more flexible that nonstretched muscles, resulting in a greater resilience to injury of the joints, ligaments, and other connective tissues. Stretching aids in muscle recovery during and following exercise. **Delayed-onset muscle soreness (DOMS)**, which can last up to 7 days after a workout, describes the muscular pain that follows intense exercise. DOMS results from damage to the muscle fibers that causes an activation of the nerve endings embedded in the damaged fibers. Stretching before and after exercise reduces the chances of muscular pain and soreness.

delayed-onset muscle soreness (DOMS) muscular pain caused by damaged muscle fibers that follows intense exercise

In a gymnasium environment it is usually the stretching component of the workout that best lends itself to psychological preparation. Ideally, stretching should be performed in a calm setting immediately prior to the main component of the workout. Stretching prior to a workout is primarily performed to lessen injuries and not to increase flexibility. Stretching exercises performed to increase flexibility should be completed after exercise when the muscles are warm and pliable.

Flexibility

The term **flexibility** refers to the possible range of movement of a joint and the extendability of the surrounding muscle structures and soft tissues. Good flexibility is an indication that there are no adhesions or abnormalities in or around a joint and that there are no serious muscular limitations. Levels of flexibility differ from person to person and are dependent on the structure of the joint, size and bulk of the muscle, level of activity participation, frequency and duration of stretching, and age and gender of the exerciser.

flexibility possible range of movement of a joint and the surrounding muscle structures

The muscle bulk of bodybuilders severely limits the flexibility of certain joints. For example, an extremely large biceps muscle will restrict the range of motion in the elbow joint. Stretching can, however, improve the flexibility of even the largest bodybuilders. Generally, individuals who frequently exercise are more flexible than those who are inactive, but certain sports are notorious for the inflexibility of their athletes, such as weight training and soccer, in which stretching is performed incorrectly or for an insufficient duration. For stretching exercises to be beneficial and to increase an individual's flexibility, the stretches must be performed on a regular basis. The frequency and duration of stretching routines differ according to the type of exercise to be performed. As a guideline, however, an individual should spend a minimum of 10 minutes prior to participating in the main activity and 5 to 10 minutes after the activity. As people age, muscular and joint structures tend to deteriorate in flexibility. Additionally, women generally are more flexible than men due to anatomical differences and the type of activities in which they participate.

flexion decreasing the angle of a joint in a folding or bending movement

extension increasing the angle of a joint in a straightening movement

abduction movement away from the body

adduction movement toward the body

The ball-and-socket joints (hip and shoulder) permit the widest range of movements in the body, namely, **flexion** (a decreasing of the angle of a joint in a folding or bending movement), **extension** (a straightening movement, which is the return from flexion), **abduction** (a movement away from the body), **adduction** (a movement toward the body), **rotation** (a pivoting movement of the bone on its own axis), and **circumduction** (a circular motion combining flexion, abduction, extension, and adduction in succession). In contrast, the hingelike

rotation a pivoting movement of the bone on its own axis

circumduction circular motion combining flexion, abduction, extension, and adduction

Figure 2.1 (on left)
Ball-and-socket joint of the hip.

Figure 2.2 (on right)
Hinge joint of the elbow.

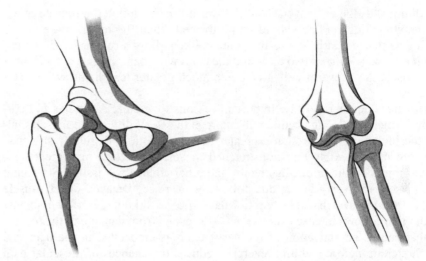

structure of the knee joint restricts movement to flexion and extension. Figures 2.1 and 2.2 show the hip and elbow joints

Active Stretching

active stretch requires the person stretching to actively supply the force

Stretching exercises can be categorized into **active stretches** and passive stretches. Active stretching requires the person to supply the force of the stretch. For example, when performing a standing quadriceps (front of upper leg) stretch on the right leg, the exerciser supplies the pulling force to lift the lower leg into position. Active stretching includes *static, ballistic,* and *dynamic* stretching, discussed below.

Static Stretching

A static stretch is the easiest and most effective active stretching technique to perform because it does not require the assistance of a partner or the use of equipment. Static stretches can be performed in the gymnasium, in the office, or in the comfort of home. A correct static stretch involves voluntary relaxation of the muscle that allows it to be simultaneously lengthened (stretched). A muscle is held in a static position at the greatest stretch possible. A force then is gradually supplied until there is a slightly uncomfortable feeling in the muscle. Once this discomfort occurs, the stretch should be maintained for approximately 15 seconds before being slowly released.

developmental stretch assists in increasing muscle and joint flexibility

As the stretching routine becomes more comfortable, the intensity of the stretch can be increased. This is achieved by applying a greater force to lengthen the muscle a little farther. Striving for an increase in flexibility is termed a **developmental stretch** and may be accompanied by a higher level of discomfort than a nondevelopmental stretch. All static stretches should be performed smoothly, slowly, and progressively. Bouncing during the stretch and forcing the muscle through too great a movement often results in muscular injury and pain.

Numerous variations of static stretching techniques exist for each body part. As previously mentioned, differences in flexibility exist between individuals, so it is important to develop a routine that incorporates the stretches that work best for each person. The following illustrations provide some examples of the most popular static stretching techniques.

■ **Chest and Shoulder**

Step 1: Stand with feet shoulder width apart, knees slightly bent, back straight, and hands joined behind the back.

Step 2: Keep the back straight and lift the hands toward the ceiling to a point where a stretch is felt in the chest. Hold for approximately 10 seconds.

■ Posterior Upper Arm

Instructions for stretching the right triceps.

Step 1: Stand with feet shoulder width apart, knees slightly bent, and back straight. Reach with the right had over the right shoulder and down the spine as far as possible.

Step 2: Place the left hand on top of the right elbow and supply light downward pressure. Hold the stretch for approximately 10 seconds. Repeat for the left triceps.

■ Anterior of Upper and Lower Arm

Instructions for stretching the right biceps and wrist flexors.

Step 1: Stand with feet shoulder width apart, knees slightly bent, and back straight. Extend the right arm in front of the body with the anterior surface of the arm upward, and place the left hand in the palm of the right.

Step 2: Supply light downward pressure with the left arm so that the stretch is felt in the wrist flexors. Hold for approximately 10 seconds. Repeat for the left biceps and wrist flexors.

■ Upper Back

Instructions for stretching the right side of the back.

Step 1: Stand with feet shoulder width apart, knees slightly bent, and back straight. Extend the right arm across the front of the body with the elbow slightly bent. Place the left hand just above the elbow of the right arm.

Step 2: Supply light pressure toward the body with the left arm. Hold for approximately 10 seconds. Repeat for left side of the back.

■ Lower Back

Step 1: Kneel on the ground and sit on the haunches, so that the buttocks touch the calf muscles. Tuck in the head and reach out along the floor with the arms.

Step 2: Reach out as far as possible for approximately 10 seconds.

■ Lower Back and Abdominals

Step 1: Lay flat on an aerobics mat in a prone position (face downward).

Step 2: Using the elbows as support, lift the upper body off the mat. Hold for approximately 10 seconds.

■ Hip Flexors and Lateral Abdominals

Instructions for stretching the right hip flexors and left lateral abdominals.

Step 1: Sit with the left leg extended and place the right foot on the outside of the left knee. Twist the upper body to the right and place the left elbow on the right knee.

Step 2: Supply light pressure with the left elbow on the right knee so that the knee is pushed across the body. Hold for approximately 10 seconds. Repeat with the other leg.

■ Groin and Lower Back

Step 1: Sit on the ground with soles of feet touching.

Step 2: Lean forward from the waist, or alternatively apply downward pressure on the knees with the hands. Hold for approximately 10 seconds.

■ Buttocks and Rear Upper Leg

Instructions for stretching the right leg.

Step 1: Lay flat on an aerobics mat in a supine position (face upward). Flex the hip so that the right leg moves toward the chest, and clasp the hands below the knee.

Step 2: Pull the knee toward the chest. Hold for approximately 10 seconds. Repeat with the left leg.

■ Front Upper Leg

Instructions for stretching the right leg.

Step 1: Lay flat on an aerobics mat in the prone position (face downward). Flex the right leg so that the heel of the right food is close to the right buttock. Clasp the foot with the right hand.

Step 2: Pull the right foot toward the buttocks with the right hand and then with both hands. Hold for approximately 10 seconds. Repeat with the left leg.

■ Rear of Upper and Lower Leg

Instructions for stretching the right leg.

Step 1: Stand with feet shoulder width apart and the right leg approximately 6 inches in front of the left. Slightly flex the left knee keeping the right leg straight.

Step 2: Lean forward with back straight and place both hands on the left knee. The stretch should be felt in the right hamstring. Lift the toes of the right foot to stretch the calf muscles. Hold for approximately 10 seconds. Repeat with the left leg.

■ Rear Lower Leg

Instructions for stretching the right leg.

Step 1: Stand facing a wall at a distance of approximately 3 feet. Step forward with the left leg and place the hands on the wall. Ensure that the left leg is bent to support the body weight.

Step 2: Keeping the right leg straight and the sole of the right foot planted on the floor, lean forward so that a stretch is felt in the calf of the right leg. To increase the stretch move further away from the wall. Hold for approximately 10 seconds. Repeat with the left leg.

Ballistic and Dynamic Stretching

ballistic stretching
active stretching technique that requires the exerciser to produce a bouncing motion

Ballistic stretching is an active stretching technique that requires the exerciser to produce a bouncing motion. As opposed to static stretching, the greatest lengthening of the muscle is not held. The object of each subsequent ballistic movement is to progressively increase the range of motion of the joint. Ballistic stretching is a less popular technique than static stretching due to the increased likelihood of muscular injury and delayed-onset muscle soreness.

Ballistic stretching is frequently performed by athletes requiring specific muscle conditioning similar to the stretching movements experience during competition. An example from track and field would be a high hurdler performing a ballistic stretching routine of the hamstrings (back of upper leg) to prepare the muscles for rapid elongation when striding the hurdles. Such sport-specific stretching is termed **dynamic stretching**. Under these circumstances the athletes usually are trained in the correct dynamic techniques and are supervised by their coaches. Dynamic stretches are always performed as part of a routine, which can include static and **proprioceptive neuromuscular facilitation (PNF)** stretches. Interestingly, research has found that static and ballistic movements produce similar gains in range of motion.

dynamic stretching amount of time spent on an exercise or workout

proprioceptive neuromuscular facilitation (PNF) the combination of the contraction and relaxation of the agonist and antagonist muscles

Passive Stretching

A **passive stretch** occurs when an external force is supplied by another individual, as with PNF stretching, or from a traction machine, such as the rack used in back injury rehabilitation. Passive stretching is uncommonly observed in a gymnasium because it requires more preparation than active stretching and often the assistance of another person.

passive stretch occurs when an external force is supplied

Proprioceptive Neuromuscular Facilitation (PNF)

The basic principal of a proprioceptive neuromuscular facilitation (PNF) stretch is the combination of the contraction and relaxation of the agonist and antagonist muscles. The nervous system reacts to the stretch by inhibiting the contraction of the agonist muscle being stretched. This results in a decrease in resistance and an increase in range of movement of the muscle. It is the role of the antagonist muscle to counteract the action of the agonist.

PNF stretches may be impractical because they require the assistance of a partner. Ideally, the individual being stretched and the individual doing the stretching should be adequately trained in the PNF stretching techniques because of the potential danger of injury. If performed correctly, however, PNF stretching will yield a greater improvement in flexibility than both the static and ballistic techniques.

There are primarily three types of PNF stretching techniques: (a) hold-relax, (b) contract-relax, and (c) slow-reversal-hold-relax. These different techniques are illustrated using three different muscle groups.

■ Hold-Relax PNF Stretching for the Chest Muscles

Step 1: Passive stretch of the chest. The subject kneels on the floor with hands behind the head. A partner stands behind and places hands on the sides of the subject, so that the upper arms of the partner rest against the elbows of the subject. The partner supplies a light resistance by forcing the subjects elbows backward (see figure 2.3, Step 1). Hold for approximately 5 seconds.

Step 2: "The push." The subject pushes lightly in a forward direction against the resistance of the partner's arms for approximately 5 seconds. The subject then pushes harder, so that the partner has to restrain the movement with increased effort (see figure 2.3, Step 2).

Step 3: Passive stretch. On the command of "relax," the subject and partner again perform a passive stretch, but with a slightly greater range of motion (see figure 2.3, Step 3). Hold for approximately 5 seconds.

Step 4: Repeat the routine for a total of 3 to 4 repetitions.

Figure 2.3

PNF stretching for the chest muscles.

■ Contract-Relax PNF Stretching for the Groin Muscles

Step 1: Passive stretch of groin (adductor muscles). The subject sits on the floor with the feet together. A partner kneels behind and places hands on the subject's knees. The partner supplies a downward pressure until the subject experiences a stretch (see figure 2.4, Step 1). Hold for approximately 5 seconds.

Step 2: Contraction of the antagonist muscles. The subject forces the knees toward the floor. The partner continues to supply a downward pressure (see figure 2.4, Step 2). Hold for approximately 5 seconds.

Step 3: Passive stretch of adductor muscles. The subject relaxes and the partner supplies a slight downward pressure to the knees (see figure 2.4, Step 3). Hold for approximately 5 seconds.

Step 4: Repeat the routine for a total of 3 to 4 repetitions.

■ Slow-Reversal-Hold-Relax PNF stretching for the Hamstrings

Step 1: Passive stretch of the hamstrings. The subject lies on the floor in a supine position (facing upward) and raises one leg to approximately 60 de-

Figure 2.4
PNF stretching for the groin muscles.

grees. When stretching the right leg, the partner places the right knee over the subject's left knee with the foot inside the subject's left ankle. The partner then places the right shoulder against the subject's right calf muscle and the right hand just below the subject's right knee. The partner then leans slightly forward until the subject feels a stretch in the right hamstrings (see figure 2.5, Step 1). Hold for approximately 5 seconds.

Step 2: Contraction of the hamstrings. The subject pushes against the shoulder of the partner for approximately 5 to 10 seconds. The partner supplies enough force to hold the leg in position (see figure 2.5, Step 2). Hold for approximately 5 to 10 seconds.

Step 3: Contraction of the quadriceps. The subject immediately contracts the quadriceps muscles and attempts to force the right foot over the head. The partner supplies a slight resistance to assist the subject (see figure 2.5, Step 3). Hold for approximately 5 to 10 seconds.

Step 4: Passive stretch of hamstrings. The subject relaxes and the partner performs a passive stretch (see figure 2.5, Step 4).

Step 5: Repeat the routine for a total of 3 to 4 repetitions.

Figure 2.5

PNF stretching for the hamstrings.

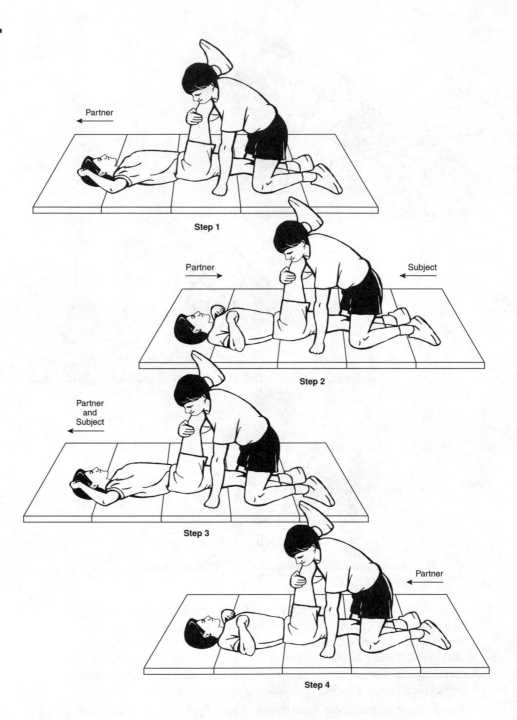

Cooldown

It is important to cool down after completing the main part of the exercise program. The term *cooldown* relates to the gradual reduction of exercise intensity. The aim of cooling down is to return the circulation and other bodily functions to as near preexercise levels as possible. Large quantities of lactic acid are produced in the blood and muscles during a workout, leading to muscle fatigue. The cooldown reduces these levels quickly by keeping the blood capillaries dilated and flushing oxygenated blood through the muscles, thereby increasing the removal of the lactic acid. The cooldown should consist of 5 to 10 minutes of light intensity exercise followed by stretching for 10 minutes. Stretching during this phase of the workout can lead to substantial increases in flexibility.

Summary

The purpose of a warm-up is to prepare muscles for the main component of the program. Without a warm-up, muscular strains and injury can occur. An exercise session should begin with a general warm-up and progress to a specific warm-up for a total of 10 to 20 minutes of warm-up time. Once the muscles are warm, a stretching routine that includes a variety of static stretching exercises should follow. The assistance of a partner significantly increases the flexibility that can be achieved through PNF stretches. To reduce muscle soreness and to increase the range of movement of a joint, a cooldown and stretching routine should follow the main exercise component. If individuals have less time than usual to workout, they should reduce the time spent on the main exercise phase. Compromising the time spent on the warm-up, stretch, and cooldown will increase the risk of injury.

WEIGHT EXERCISES FOR THE UPPER BODY

After reading this section, the student will be able to do the following:

- Perform a variety of weight training exercises for the upper body
- Identify the major muscle groups involved in the performance of each upper-body exercise

This section of the text provides examples of some of the most popular weight training exercises used to develop the upper body. Each exercise is depicted by a diagram showing the muscles used, a description of the correct technique, and an illustration of the exercise. Some of the exercises can be performed only with free weights or with weight machines, whereas others can be performed with both. Some utilize the body's own weight as resistance or alternatively can be performed using a load provided by objects commonly found in the home. These latter exercises are of particular benefit when a fitness center is inaccessible because of financial, time, or social constraints. It is vitally important that the exercises form part of a total workout routine, including the warm-up and stretching before and cooldown and stretching after the resistance exercises.

EMPHASIS 1 Back

1. Lat Pull-down (machine)

Option 1: Machine: seated (easy)

■ **Phase 1: Start (see figure 2.6)**

- Hold the bar with a pronated grip.
- Place the hands an equal distance from the center and approximately shoulder width or greater apart.
- Keep the back straight.
- Face the machine, and position the center of the bar above the back of the neck.

■ **Phase 2: Downward (see figure 2.7)**

- Pull the bar slowly downward behind the neck.
- Don't force the bar against the top of the spine.
- Alternatively, dip the bar to the front.
- Exhale on the downward motion.

Figure 2.6 (on left)
Lat pull-down: starting
position.

Figure 2.7 (on right)
Lat pull-down: downward
motion.

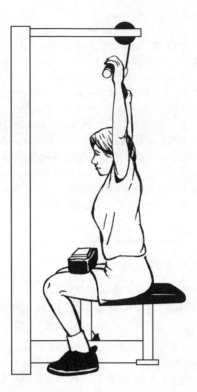

Figure 2.8

Lat pull-down: kneeling
position.

■ **Phase 3: Upward**

- Control the movement by slowly returning the bar to the starting position.
- Inhale on the upward motion.

Option 2: Machine: kneeling (see figure 2.8)

2. Seated Row (machine)

Option 1: Machine—seated

■ **Phase 1: Start (see figure 2.9)**

- Sit on the floor, with the legs extended so that the feet rest on the foot supports.
- Bend the knees slightly.
- Grip the handles so the hands are close together.
- Keep the back straight by pivoting from the waist.
- Keep arms slightly flexed at the elbows.

■ **Phase 2: Backward (see figure 2.10)**

- Keeping the back straight and legs slightly bent, flex the arms bringing the handles to a position just below the chest.
- Make sure that the wire from the machine remains parallel to the incline bench brought back above the chest.
- Keep the elbows close to the body.
- Exhale on the backward motion.

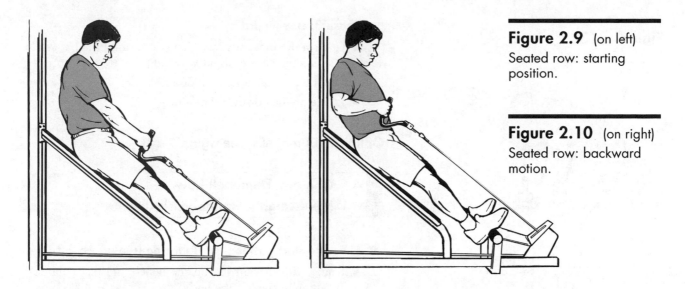

Figure 2.9 (on left)
Seated row: starting position.

Figure 2.10 (on right)
Seated row: backward motion.

■ **Phase 3: Forward**

- Return the handles to the starting position in a slow and controlled manner.
- Keep the back straight and the knees bent throughout the exercise.
- Inhale on the forward motion.

3. Bent-over Row (free weights—barbell and dumbbells)

Option 1: Barbell

■ **Phase 1: Start (see figure 2.11)**

- Hold the bar with a pronated grip.
- Place the hands an equal distance from the center and approximately shoulder width apart.
- Bend at the waist so the chest is over the bar.
- Keep the back flat and in a stationary position.
- Flex the knees.

■ **Phase 2: Upward (see figure 2.12)**

- Lift the bar from the floor to the chest, concentrating on keeping the back flat.
- Force the elbows toward the ceiling.
- Exhale on the upward motion.
- Touch the bar to the lower chest.

Figure 2.11 (on left)
Bent-over row: starting position.

Figure 2.12 (on right)
Bent-over row: upward motion.

Figure 2.13

Bent-over row with dumbbells.

■ **Phase 3: Downward**

- Control the movement by slowly returning the bar while keeping the elbows slightly flexed.
- Don't let the bar touch the floor.
- Inhale on the downward motion.

Option 2: Dumbbells (see figure 2.13)

> 4. **One-arm Dumbbell Row (free weights—dumbbells)**

■ **Phase 1: Start position for right side (see figure 2.14)**

- Kneel with the left leg on the bench and place the left hand out to support the body.
- Place the right foot to the side of the bench with the right knee slightly flexed.
- Hold the dumbbell with the right hand.
- Keep the back flat and parallel to the floor.

■ **Phase 2: Upward (see figure 2.15)**

- Lift the dumbbell toward the right side of the chest.
- Keep the elbows close to the side of the body.
- Exhale on the upward motion.
- Restrict the amount of arm involvement.

■ **Phase 3: Downward**

- Control the movement by slowly returning the dumbbell while keeping the elbow slightly flexed.
- Don't let the dumbbell touch the floor.
- Inhale on the downward motion.

Figure 2.14 (on left)

One-arm dumbbell row: starting position.

Figure 2.15 (on right)

One-arm dumbbell row: upward motion.

5. Upright Row (free weights—barbell, dumbbells)

Option: Barbell

■ **Phase 1: Start (see figure 2.16)**

- Place the hands approximately 4 inches apart on the bar.
- Place the feet shoulder width apart with the knees slightly flexed.
- Hold the bar with a pronated grip and a slight flexion of the elbows.
- Keep the back straight.

■ **Phase 2: Upward (see figure 2.17)**

- Lift the bar upward to a position just under the chin.
- Keep the bar close to the body at all times.
- Keep the elbows higher than the bar.
- Exhale on the upward motion.

■ **Phase 3: Downward**

- Control the movement by slowly returning the bar downward while keeping the elbows slightly flexed.
- Inhale on the downward motion.

Figure 2.16 (on left)
Upright row: starting position.

Figure 2.17 (on right)
Upright row: upward motion.

Figure 2.18

Upright dumbbell row.

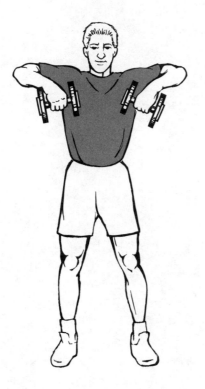

Option 2: Dumbbells (see figure 2.18)

- Ensure that both hands are level during the lifting phases.
- Don't jerk backward to assist in the lift.

6. Shoulder Shrugs (free weights— barbell and dumbbells)

Option 1: Barbell

- **Phase 1: Start (see figure 2.19)**
  - Place the hands approximately body width apart on the bar.
  - Place the feet shoulder width apart with the knees slightly flexed.
  - Maintain a slight flexion in the elbows.
  - Keep the back straight.

- **Phase 2: Upward (see figure 2.20)**
  - Shrug the shoulders forward toward the ears.
  - Exhale on the upward motion.

- **Phase 3: Downward**
  - Control the movement by slowly returning the bar downward.
  - Inhale on the downward motion.

Figure 2.19 (on left)

Shoulder shrugs: starting position.

Figure 2.20 (on right)

Shoulder shrugs: upward motion.

Option 2: Dumbbells (see figure 2.21)

- Ensure both hands are level during the lifting phases.
- Don't jerk backward to assist in the lift.

7. Lower-back Raises (body resistance)*

■ Phase 1: Start (see figure 2.22)

- Lie in a prone position (face downward) on the ground.
- Place the hands to the side of the head, so that the elbows point away from the body.
- Keep the toes in contact with the surface of the mat.

■ Phase 2: Upward (see figure 2.23)

- Using the muscles in the lower back, slowly lift the upper body away from the mat.
- Lift as high as is comfortable.
- Exhale on the upward motion.

■ Phase 3: Downward

- Control the movement by slowly returning the upper body toward the mat.
- Inhale on the downward motion.

Figure 2.21
Shoulder shrugs with dumbbells.

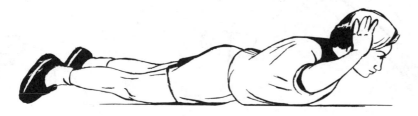

Figure 2.22
Lower-back raises: starting position.

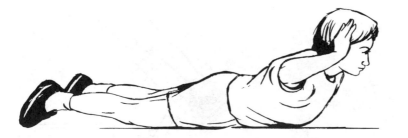

Figure 2.23
Lower-back raises: upward motion.

*Note: This exercise is ideal for a beginner to develop the basic strength to perform the lower back hyperextensions. However, it does not train the erectors through their full range of motion.

8. Lower-back Hyperextensions (machine/body resistance)**

■ Phase 1: Start (see figure 2.24)

- Lie in a prone position (face downward) on the hyperextension bench.
- Place the hands to the side of the head, so that the elbows point away from the body.
- Keep the thighs and calves in contact with the padded surfaces of the machine.
- Allow the upper body to hang at 90 degrees to the hip.

■ Phase 2: Upward (see figure 2.25)

- Raise the upper body to a comfortable position. Ideally the upper body should hyperextend.
- Exhale on the upward motion.

■ Phase 3: Downward

- Control the movement by slowly returning the upper body to the starting position.
- Exhale on the upward motion.

Figure 2.24 (on left)
Lower-back hyperextension: starting position.

Figure 2.25 (on right)
Lower-back hyperextension: upward motion.

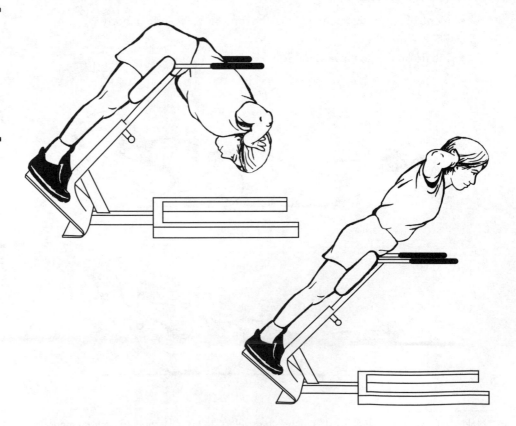

**Note: This exercise should not be performed by individuals suffering from spinal disorders unless prescribed by a physician.

EMPHASIS 2 | Shoulders

9. Front Dumbbell Raises (free weights)

■ **Phase 1: Start (see figure 2.26)**

- Hold the dumbbells with a pronated grip.
- Stand with the feet shoulder width apart and knees slightly flexed.
- Stand relaxed with the weights resting against the thigh.
- Keep the elbows slightly flexed.
- Keep the back straight.

■ **Phase 2: Upward (see figure 2.27)**

- Keeping the elbows slightly flexed, lift the weight so that it is level to the shoulder.
- Maintain a 90 degree angle between the body and arms.
- Don't lean backward to force the weight upward.
- Exhale on the upward motion.

■ **Phase 3: Downward**

- Control the movement by slowly returning the dumbbells to the starting position.
- Inhale on the downward motion.

  Note: This exercise should not be performed by individuals suffering from spinal disorders unless prescribed by a physician.

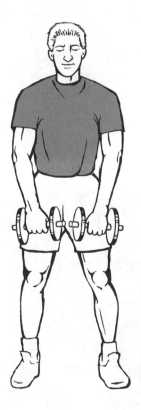

Figure 2.26 (on left)
Front raises: starting position.

Figure 2.27 (on right)
Front raises: upward motion.

10. Shoulder press (machine, free weights— barbell and dumbbells)

Option 1: Machine

■ **Phase 1: Start (see figure 2.28)**

- Sit on the seat facing forward.
- Grip the handles with a pronated grip.
- Maintain a slight flexion in the elbows.
- Keep the back straight.

■ **Phase 2: Upward (see figure 2.29)**

- Push upward from the shoulders, not from the back.
- Continue to lift until the arms are slightly flexed.
- Exhale on the upward motion.

■ **Phase 3: Downward**

- Control the movement by slowly returning the handles to a position just above the shoulders.
- Inhale on the downward motion.

Option 2: Dumbbells (see figure 2.30)

- Ensure both weights remain level.
- Don't jerk backwards to assist in the lift.

Option 3: Barbell

- Keep the bar parallel to the floor throughout the movement.
- Use a spotter, if necessary.

Figure 2.28 (on left)
Shoulder press: starting position.

Figure 2.29 (on right)
Shoulder press: upward motion.

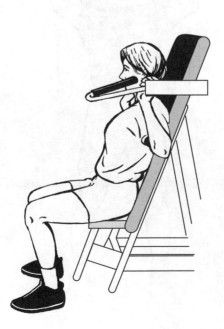

11. Deltoid Raises (machine)

■ Phase 1: Start (see figure 2.31)

- Sit in the machine with the back pressed against the support.
- Adjust the padded rollers to shoulder level.
- Place the arms around the rollers and grip over the top.
- Keep the back straight.

■ Phase 2: Upward (see figure 2.32)

- Lift the arms upward using the deltoid muscles.
- Exhale on the upward motion.

■ Phase 3: Downward

- Control the movement by slowly returning the rollers to the starting position.
- Inhale on the downward motion.

EMPHASIS   3   Chest

12. Bench Press

■ Phase 1: Start (see figure 2.33)

- Lie on the bench so that the chest is in line with the bar.
- Place the feet either on the floor or on the edge of the bench.
- Grip the bar with a pronated grip.
- Press the head, back, and buttocks flat against the bench.
- Flex the elbows.

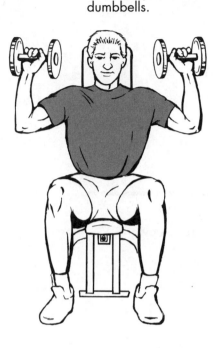

Figure 2.30
Shoulder press with dumbbells.

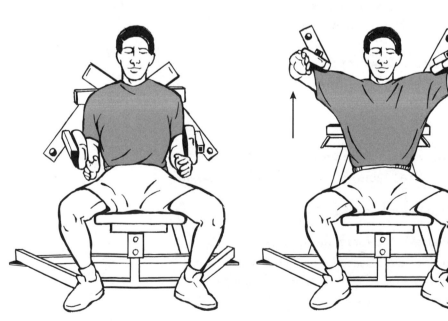

Figure 2.31 (on left)
Deltoid raises: starting position.

Figure 2.32 (on right)
Deltoid raises: upward motion.

Figure 2.33

Bench press: starting position.

Figure 2.34

Bench press: upward motion.

■ **Phase 2: Upward (see figure 2.34)**

- Lift the bar off the supports, pushing upward.
- Don't lock the elbows.
- Exhale on the upward motion.

■ **Phase 3: Downward**

- Control the movement by slowly returning the bar to the starting position.
- Inhale on the downward motion.

13. Flat, incline, and decline chest press (free weights—barbell and dumbbells)

Option 1: Barbell—Flat Bench

■ **Phase 1: Start (see figure 2.35)**

- Lie on the bench so that the chest is in line with the barbell.
- Place the feet either on the floor or on the edge of the bench.
- Grip the bar with a pronated grip.

Figure 2.35
Flat-bench barbell chest press: starting position.

- Press the head, back, and buttocks flat against the bench.
- Flex the elbows.

■ Phase 2: Upward

- Lift the weight off the supports, pushing upward. (The use of a spotter is advised.)
- Exhale on the upward motion.

■ Phase 3: Downward (see figure 2.36)

- Control the movement by slowly returning the bar to a position just above the chest.
- Inhale on the downward motion.

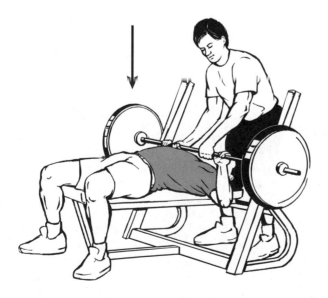

Figure 2.36
Flat-bench barbell chest press: downward motion.

Figure 2.37
Incline barbell chest
press.

Option 2: Incline Chest Press with Barbell—Upper Chest (see figure 2.37)

- Keep the barbell level.
- Don't jerk backward to assist in the lift.

Option 3: Decline Chest Press with Barbell—Lower Chest (see figure 2.38)

- Tilt the bench to the decline position.
- Secure the body by placing feet over the leg supports.
- Use a spotter, if necessary.

Option 4: Dumbbells (see figure 2.39)

- Keep the weights level.
- Use a spotter, if necessary.
- Perform alternatively at an incline or decline, if desired.

Figure 2.38
Decline barbell chest
press.

14. Dumbbell Chest Fly (free weights)

■ **Phase 1: Start (see figure 2.40)**

- Lie on the bench with the feet either on the floor or on the edge of the bench.
- Grip the weights with a pronated grip.
- Hold the weights above the chest and rotate the hands so that the weights face each other.
- Press the head, back, and buttocks flat against the bench.
- Flex the elbows.

Figure 2.39 (on left)
Flat dumbbell chest press.

Figure 2.40 (on right)
Dumbbell chest fly:
starting position.

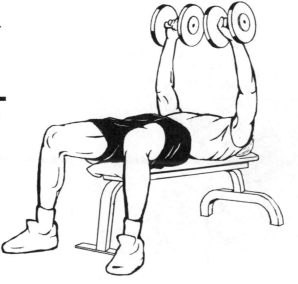
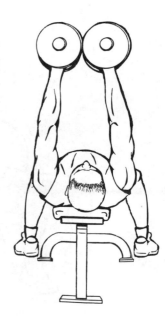

Figure 2.41
Dumbbell chest fly:
outward motion.

■ Phase 2: Outward (see figure 2.41)

- Move the weights outward in an arc, until they are level with the chest.
- Keep the weights level.
- Inhale on the outward motion.

■ Phase 3: Inward

- Control the movement by slowly returning the weights in an arc back to the starting position.
- Exhale on the inward motion.

15. Pec Deck (machine)

■ Phase 1: Start (see figure 2.42)

- Sit in the seat with the back flat against the support.
- Adjust the seat so the handles are level with the chest.
- Place the hands and forearms against the pads.
- Hold the elbows parallel to the shoulders.

■ Phase 2: Forward (see figure 2.43)

- Push forward so that the pads meet in front of the chest.
- Direct effort through the elbows and not through the hands.
- Exhale on the forward motion.

■ Phase 3: Backward

- Control the movement by slowly returning the handles to the starting position.
- Inhale on the backward motion.

Figure 2.42
Pec deck: starting position.

Figure 2.43

Peck deck: forward motion.

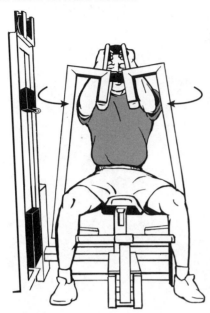

EMPHASIS 4 Front of Upper Arm

16. Biceps Curl (free weights— dumbbells and barbells)

Option 1: Seated Dumbbell Curl

■ **Phase 1: Start (see figure 2.44)**

- Sit with the back flat against the support.
- Place the soles of the feet on the floor.
- Hold the dumbbells with a supinated grip, with the palms facing forward.
- Let the weights freely suspend to the side of the body.

■ **Phase 2: Upward (see figure 2.45)**

- Raise the dumbbell(s) in an arc toward the shoulder(s).
- Control the movement, without swinging.
- Keep the elbows tucked to the side of the body.
- Exhale on the upward motion.
- Lift both weights together or alternately.

■ **Phase 3: Downward**

- Control the movement by slowly returning the weights to the starting position.
- Inhale on the downward motion.

Option 2: Standing Dumbbell Curl (see figure 2.46)

- Keep the back straight: don't arch it to force the weights up.

Option 3: Standing Barbell Curl

- Keep the bar level throughout the exercise.

Figure 2.44 (on left)

Seated biceps curl: starting position.

Figure 2.45 (on right)

Seated biceps curl: upward motion.

17. Biceps Concentration Curl (free weights—dumbbells)

■ Phase 1: Start (see figure 2.47)

- Sit on the one side of the bench with feet flat on the floor.
- Lean forward at the waist so that the shoulders are above the knees.
- Place the right elbow inside the right knee.
- Pick up the dumbbell with a supinated grip.
- Keep the back flat.

■ Phase 2: Upward (see figure 2.48)

- Lift the weight toward the chest, flexing and pivoting at the elbow.
- Use the left hand to assist by supporting below the right elbow.
- Don't arch the back to raise the weight.
- Exhale on the upward motion.

■ Phase 3: Downward

- Control the movement by slowly returning the weight to the start position.
- Inhale on the downward motion.

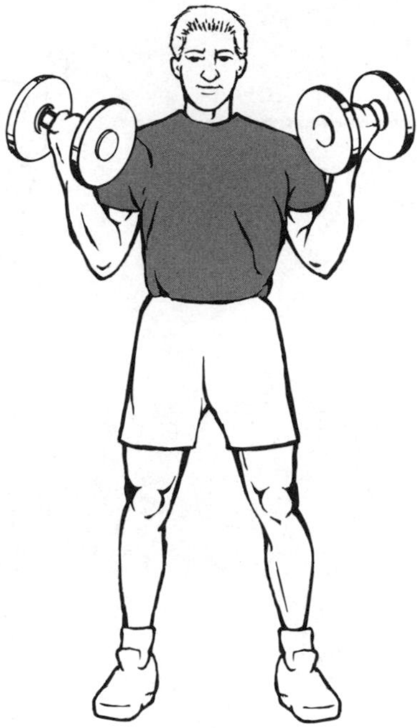

18. Preacher Curl (machine and free weights—barbell)

Option 1: Machine Preacher Curl

■ Phase 1: Start (see figure 2.49)

- Sit facing the machine with the upper arms on the padded surface.
- Pick up the bar with a supinated grip, keeping the elbows slightly flexed.
- Keep the back straight.

Figure 2.46
Standing biceps curl with dumbbells.

Figure 2.47 (on left)
Biceps concentration curl: starting position.

Figure 2.48 (on right)
Biceps concentration curl: upward position.

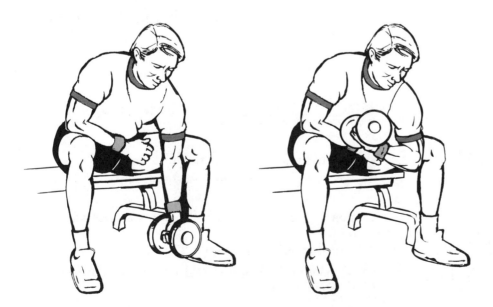

Figure 2.49 (on left)
Preacher curl: starting
position.

Figure 2.50 (on right)
Preacher curl: upward
motion.

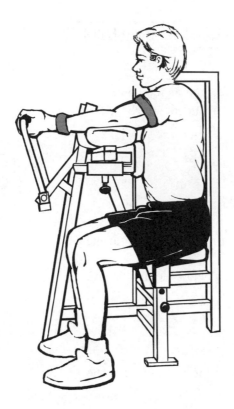

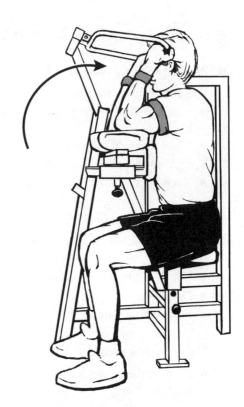

■ **Phase 2: Upward (see figure 2.50)**

■ Lift the bar toward the chest by flexing at the elbows.

■ Exhale on the upward motion.

■ **Phase 3: Downward**

■ Control movement by slowly returning the bar to the starting position.

■ Inhale on the downward motion.

Figure 2.51

Preacher curl with a
barbell.

Option 2: Barbell Preacher Curl (see figure 2.51)

■ Keep the back straight. Don't arch the back to force the weight up.

■ Keep the bar level at all times.

EMPHASIS **5** **Back of Upper Arm**

19. Triceps Extension (machine and free weights—barbell and dumbbells)

Option 1: Standing Dumbbell Extension (right triceps)

■ **Phase 1: Start (see figure 2.52)**

■ Stand with the feet shoulder width apart and the knees slightly flexed.

- Hold the dumbbell in the palm of the right hand and grip it tightly.
- Lift the right arm so the elbow is adjacent to the right side of the head.
- Flex the arm so that the weight is suspended behind the right shoulder.

■ Phase 2: Upward (see figure 2.53)

- Extend the right arm, keeping the upper arm stationary and close to the side of the head.
- Exhale on the upward motion.
- Don't allow any lateral movement of the upper arm.

■ Phase 3: Downward

- Control the movement by slowly returning the weight to the starting position.
- Inhale on the downward motion.
- Work the left triceps in a similar manner.

Option 2: Barbell Triceps Extension (see figure 2.54)

- Work both arms at the same time with a comfortable grip on the bar.

Option 3: Triceps Extension—Machine (see figure 2.55)

- Sit facing the machine and grip the handles.
- Elbows should be the same height as the shoulders.
- Fully extend the arms.
- Slowly return the handles to the starting position.

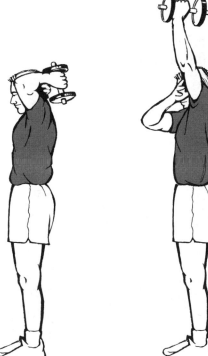

Figure 2.52 (on left)
Triceps extension: starting position.

Figure 2.53 (center)
Triceps extension: upward motion.

Figure 2.54 (on right)
Triceps extension with a barbell.

Figure 2.55

Triceps extensions on a machine.

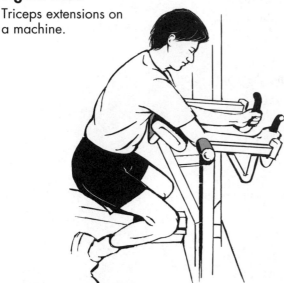

20. Triceps Dip (body resistance)

■ **Phase 1: Start (see figure 2.56)**
- Grip the sides of an aerobics box or bench.
- Place the hands shoulder width apart.
- Extend the legs so that the body is supported by the arms and feet.
- Fully extend the arms.

■ **Phase 2: Downward (see figure 2.57)**
- Flex the arms, lowering the upper body toward the floor.
- Inhale on the downward motion.

■ **Phase 3: Upward**
- Extend the arms pushing the upper body in an upward direction.
- Exhale on the upward motion.

21. Lying Triceps Extension (free weights—dumbbells and barbell)

Option 1: Barbell

■ **Phase 1: Start (see figure 2.58)**
- Lay in a supine position on the bench so that the head rests at the end of the bench.
- Press the head, back, and buttocks flat against the bench.
- Grasp the bar with a pronated grip, hands shoulder width apart.
- Position the bar with arms extended above the head.

Figure 2.56 (on left)

Triceps dip: starting position.

Figure 2.57 (on right)

Triceps dip: downward motion.

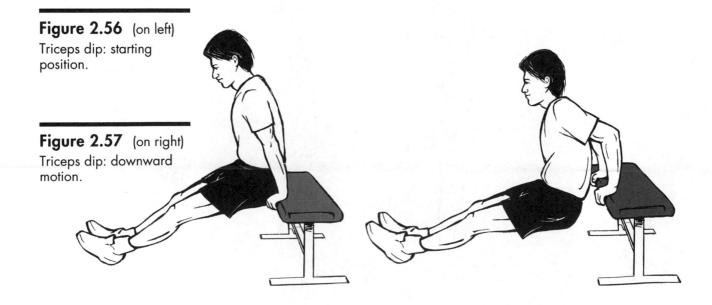

■ Phase 2: Downward (see figure 2.59)

- Keeping the elbows parallel to the forehead, flex the elbows, allowing the bar to move behind the head.
- Inhale on the downward motion.

■ Phase 3: Upward

- Extend the arms so that the bar returns to the starting position.
- Exhale on the upward motion.

Option 2: Dumbbell (see figure 2.60)

- Hold one dumbbell between two hands.
- Don't swing the weight.
- Ensure the dumbbell is well maintained prior to lifting the weight above the head.

22. Triceps Pushdown (machine)

■ Phase 1: Start (see figure 2.61)

- Stand facing the machine with the feet shoulder width apart and knees slightly flexed.
- Place the hands 6 to 10 inches apart with a pronated grip.
- Tuck the elbows close to the side of the body.
- Hold the handle level with the chest.

■ Phase 2: Downward (see figure 2.62)

- Keeping the elbow close to the side, extend the arms by pushing the hands downward.
- Exhale on the downward motion.

■ Phase 3: Upward

- Control the return of the handle to the starting position.
- Inhale on the upward motion.

EMPHASIS   6   Forearms

23. Wrist Curl (free weights—barbell)

■ Phase 1: Start (see figure 2.63)

- Sit on the end of the bench.
- Lift the bar with a supinated grip, with the hands 6 to 8 inches apart.

Figure 2.58
Lying triceps extension: starting position.

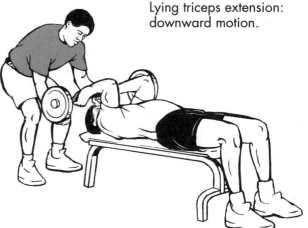

Figure 2.59
Lying triceps extension: downward motion.

Figure 2.60
Lying triceps extension with a dumbbell.

Figure 2.61 (on left)
Triceps pushdown:
starting position.

Figure 2.62 (on right)
Triceps pushdown:
downward motion.

- Lean forward, balancing the forearms on the thighs.
- Allow the wrists to hang over the knees.

■ **Phase 2: Upward (see figure 2.64)**
- With the palms upward, flex the wrists and lift the bar upward.
- Keep the forearms on the thighs.
- Exhale on the upward motion.

Figure 2.63 (on left)
Wrist curl: starting
position.

Figure 2.64 (on right)
Wrist curl: upward
motion.

■ Phase 3: Downward

- Open the palms and allow the bar to roll down them to the finger tips and return to the starting position.
- Inhale on the downward motion.

24. Wrist Extension (free weights—barbell)

■ Phase 1: Start (see figure 2.65)

- Sit on the end of the bench.
- Lift the bar with a pronated grip, with the hands 6 to 8 inches apart.
- Lean forward, balancing the forearms on the thighs.
- Allow the wrists to hang over the knees.

■ Phase 2: Upward (see figure 2.66)

- With the palms downward, extend the wrists and lift the bar toward the body. Forearms remain on the thighs.
- Exhale on the upward motion.

■ Phase 3: Downward

- Flex the wrist in a slow and controlled manner and return the bar to the starting position.
- Inhale on the downward motion.

Figure 2.65 (on left)
Wrist extension: starting position.

Figure 2.66 (on right)
Wrist extension: upward motion.

EMPHASIS | **7** | **Abdominals**

25. Bent-knee Sit-up (body resistance)

- ■ **Phase 1: Start (see figure 2.67)**
  - Lie in a supine position (face upward) on an aerobics mat.
  - Place the hands to the side of the head, so that the elbows point away from the body.
  - Bend the knees so that the back and soles of the feet are flat against the mat.

- ■ **Phase 2: Upward (see figure 2.68)**
  - Using the abdominal muscles, slowly lift the upper body off the mat.
  - Lift until a contraction is felt in the abdominals.
  - Exhale on the upward motion.
  - Increase the intensity by placing the hands above and away from the head.

- ■ **Phase 3: Downward**
  - Control the movement by slowly returning the upper body toward the mat.
  - Don't allow the shoulders to touch the mat prior to starting the next repetition.
  - Inhale on the downward motion.

Figure 2.67

Bent-knee sit-up: starting position.

Figure 2.68

Bent-knee sit-up: upward motion.

26. Twist Sit-up (body resistance)

■ Phase 1: Start (see figure 2.69)

- Lie in a supine position (face upward) on an aerobics mat.
- Place the hands to the side of the head, so that the elbows point away from the body.
- Bend the left knee so that the back is flat against the mat, and place the right foot on the left knee so that the right knee points away from the body.

■ Phase 2: Upward (see figure 2.70)

- Using the abdominal muscles, lift the upper body off the mat and twist toward the right knee.
- Lift until a contraction is felt in the abdominals.
- Exhale on the upward motion.
- Increase the intensity by placing the hands above and away from the head.

■ Phase 3: Downward

- Control the movement by slowly returning the upper body toward the mat.
- Don't allow the shoulders to touch the mat prior to starting the next repetition.
- Inhale on the downward motion.
- Repeat the movement sequence on the other side.

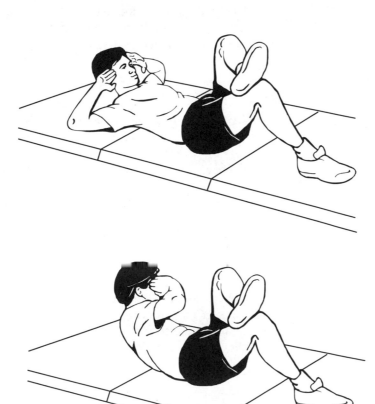

Figure 2.69
Twist sit-up: starting position.

Figure 2.70
Twist sit-up: upward motion.

Figure 2.71

Incline sit-up: starting position.

Figure 2.72

Incline sit-up: upward motion.

27. Incline Sit-up (body resistance)

■ Phase 1: Start (see figure 2.71)

- Lie in a supine position (face upward) on a bench with a slight incline.
- Place the hands to the side of the head, so that the elbows point away from the body.
- Place the legs over the padded roller to secure the body in position. Flex the knees so that the back and buttocks are flat on the bench.

■ Phase 2: Upward (see figure 2.72)

- Using the abdominal muscles, slowly lift the upper off the bench.
- Lift until a contraction is felt in the abdominals.
- Exhale on the upward motion.
- Increase the intensity by placing the hands above and away from the head.

■ Phase 3: Downward

- Control the movement by slowly returning the upper body toward the bench.
- Don't allow the shoulders to touch the bench prior to starting the next repetition.
- Inhale on the downward motion.

Summary

This section introduced a variety of exercises for the upper body that can be performed safely by either an experienced or novice weight lifter. One exercise should be selected for each body part for a total fitness training program. To fulfill a specific objective, such as increasing the strength of the biceps, two or three bicept exercises may be required. The choice of exercises depends on such factors as experience and personal goals, but generally it is safer for an inexperienced weight trainer to begin with exercises that are performed on machines.

The lifter should be cautious when attempting new exercises, however, and attend to both personal safety and that of other exercisers in the vicinity. Before attempting an exercise observed in the gymnasium or read about in a magazine, the exerciser should consult a personal trainer regarding correct lifting techniques. An inexperienced weight lifter should master the correct techniques with the machine exercises before attempting the free-weight exercises.

After reading this section, the student will be able to do the following:

- Perform a variety of weight training exercises for the lower body.
- Identify the major muscle groups involved in the performance of each lower-body exercise.

This section of the text provides examples of the most popular weight training exercises used to develop the three major muscle groups of the lower body: the quadriceps (front of upper leg), the hamstrings (back of upper leg), and the gastrocnemius (back of lower leg). The quadriceps and hamstrings are two of the largest muscle groups of the body and are capable of lifting extremely heavy loads. Often the hamstrings are neglected when training, which often leads to injury because of a muscle imbalance with the quadriceps. The reasons for focusing solely on exercising the quadriceps include short-term noticeable increases in strength and muscle size compared with the hamstring and the gastrocnemius muscles. Working the hamstrings is not only important in the prevention of injury, but also will lead to greater strength potential in the legs and all-around muscular definition.

Due to the heavy loads that can be lifted by the legs, the majority of leg exercises are performed on machines that allow greater weights to be lifted in a relatively safe environment. Some of the exercises described can be performed using the body's own weight as resistance or with a load provided by objects commonly found in the home. These exercises will be of particular benefit when the facilities of a fitness center are inaccessible because of financial, time, or social constraints. It is vitally important that the exercises form part of a total workout routine, including warming up and stretching before and after the exercises.

EMPHASIS 8 | Legs

1. Leg Extension (machine)

- **Phase 1: Start (see figure 2.73)**
  - Sit in the machine.
  - Lie with the back flat against the support.
  - Place the feet under the roller pads.
  - Spread the legs approximately shoulder width apart.
  - Align the knees with the axis of the machine.

- **Phase 2: Upward (see figure 2.74)**
  - Fully extend the legs, lifting the weight of the stack.
  - Press backward with the buttocks and the back.
  - Exhale on the upward motion.

- **Phase 3: Downward**
  - Lower the weight slowly and with control.
  - Inhale on the downward motion.

Figure 2.73 (on left)
Leg extension: starting position.

Figure 2.74 (on right)
Leg extension: upward motion.

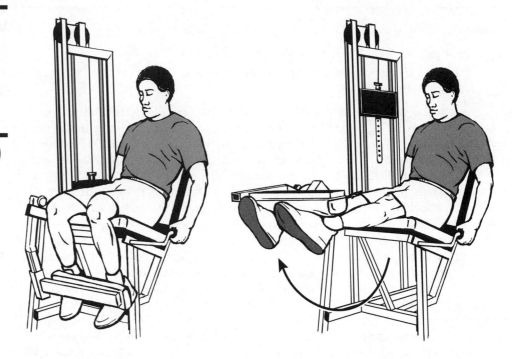

2. Leg Press (machine)

■ **Phase 1: Start (see figure 2.75)**

- Sit in the machine.
- Push the back flat against the support.
- Place the feet on the foot pedals.
- Spread the legs approximately shoulder width apart.

■ **Phase 2: Forward (see figure 2.76)**

- Extend the legs, pushing the pedals toward the machine, until there is a slight flexion in the legs.
- Press backward with the buttocks and the back.
- Exhale on the forward motion.

Figure 2.75
Leg press: starting position.

Figure 2.76

Leg press: forward motion.

■ **Phase 3: Backward**

- Lower the weight slowly and with control.
- Inhale on the backward motion.

3. Squat (free weights—barbell)

■ **Phase 1: Start (see figure 2.77)**

- With a pronated grip, grasp the bar with the hands just over shoulder width apart.
- Step under the bar and rest it on the top of the trapezius.
- Stand with legs slightly flexed and the feet shoulder width apart.
- Ensure that the bar does not rest on the spine.

■ **Phase 2: Downward (see figure 2.78)**

- Slowly lower the bar by flexing the knees and hips.
- Keep the back straight.
- Bear the weight on the feet, not on the toes.
- Lower the body until the thighs are just above a parallel position to the ground.
- Inhale on the downward motion.
- Use a spotter for the squat.

■ **Phase 3: Upward**

- Slowly rise by straightening the legs.
- Keep the knees aligned with the feet.
- Exhale on the upward motion.

Figure 2.77

Squat: starting position.

Figure 2.78
Squat: downward motion.

4. Lunge (free weights—barbell)

■ **Phase 1: Start (see figure 2.79)**

- With a pronated grip, grasp the bar with the hands shoulder width apart.
- Lift the bar over the head and rest it on the top of the trapezius.
- Stand with the legs slightly flexed and the feet shoulder width apart.

■ **Phase 2: Forward (see figure 2.80)**

- Take a large step forward with one leg.
- Plant the lead leg.
- Flex the lead leg and then lower the trailing leg toward the floor.
- Lower the body until the leading thigh is just above a parallel position to the ground.
- Inhale on the forward motion.
- Use a spotter for the lunge.

■ **Phase 3: Backward**

- Forcefully drive backward off the lead leg.
- Keep the knees in alignment with the feet and the back straight.
- Exhale on the backward motion.

Figure 2.79 (on left)
Lunge: starting position.

Figure 2.80 (on right)
Lunge: forward motion.

5. Leg Curl (machine)

■ Phase 1: Start (see figure 2.81)

- Lie in a prone position (face down) on the machine.
- Press the hips and chest flat.
- Position the knees just below the edge of the pad.
- Position the ankles under the roller pads.
- Align the knees with the axis of the machine.

■ Phase 2: Upward (see figure 2.82)

- Flex the legs to bring the roller up toward the buttocks.
- Exhale on the upward movement.

■ Phase 3: Downward

- Lower the weight slowly and with control.
- Inhale on the downward motion.

6. Calf Raise (machine)

■ Phase 1: Start (see figure 2.83)

- Position the padded shoulder supports on top of the left and right shoulders.
- Stand with the feet shoulder width apart with the balls of the feet on the edge of the raised step.
- Lift the weight off the stack by extending the knees.

■ Phase 2: Upward (see figure 2.84)

- Push up on to the toes as high as possible lifting the weights away from the stack.
- Exhale on the upward motion.

■ Phase 3: Downward

- Lower the heels below the surface of step and the toes.
- Keep the knees in alignment with the feet.
- Inhale on the downward motion.

Figure 2.81
Leg curl: starting position.

Figure 2.82
Leg curl: upward motion.

Figure 2.83 (on left)
Calf raise: starting
position.

Figure 2.84 (on right)
Calf raise: upward
motion.

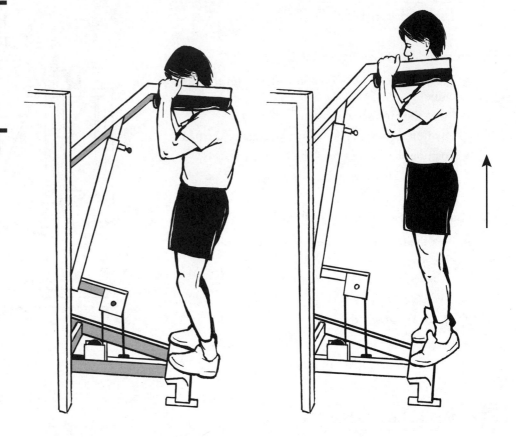

7. Toe Raise (machine)

■ **Phase 1: Start (see figure 2.85)**

- Sit on the seat and place the thighs (just above the knee) under the padded supports.
- Align the knees with the ankles.
- Place the hands on the handles provided and support the lift.
- Lift the weight by pushing downward with the toes, forcing the knees upward.

■ **Phase 2: Upward (see figure 2.86)**

- Push up on the toes as high as possible, lifting the weights away from the stack.
- Exhale on the upward motion.

■ **Phase 3: Downward**

- Lower the heels below the surface of step and the toes.
- Keep the knees in alignment with the feet.
- Inhale on the downward motion.

Figure 2.85 (on left)
Toe raise: starting position.

Figure 2.86 (on right)
Toe raise: upward motion.

8. Leg Adduction (machine)

■ **Phase 1: Start (see figure 2.87)**
- Sit on the machine with the back pressed firmly against the back support.
- Place the legs in the leg braces.
- Adjust the machine according to degree of flexibility.
- Place the hands on the handles provided.

■ **Phase 2: Inward (see figure 2.88)**
- Force the legs together in a slow and controlled manner, lifting weights off the stack.
- Exhale on the inward movement.

■ **Phase 3: Outward**
- In a slow and controlled motion, lower the weights by allowing the legs to return to the starting position.
- Inhale on the outward motion.

Figure 2.87

Leg adduction: starting position.

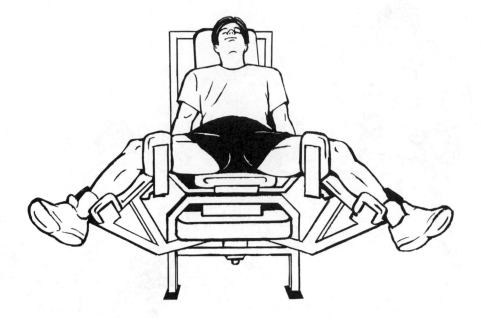

Figure 2.88

Leg adduction: inward motion.

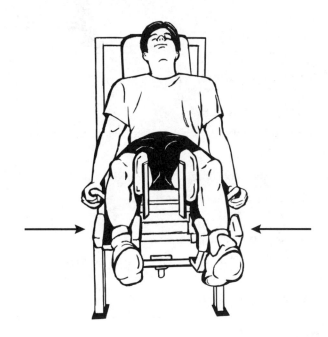

9. Leg abduction (machine)

■ **Phase 1: Start (see figure 2.89)**

- Sit on the machine with the back pressed firmly against the back support.
- Place the legs in the leg braces.
- Adjust the machine according to degree of flexibility.
- Place the hands on the handles provided.

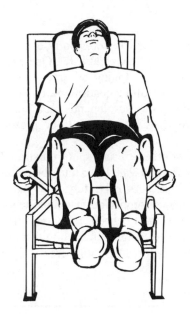

Figure 2.89
Leg abduction: starting position.

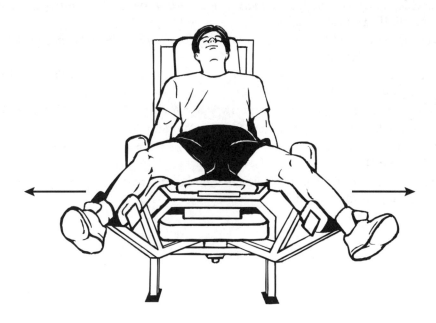

Figure 2.90
Leg abduction: outward motion.

■ Phase 2: Outward (see figure 2.90)

- Force the legs apart in a slow and controlled manner, lifting the weights off the stack.
- Exhale on the outward movement.

■ Phase 3: Inward

- In a slow and controlled motion, lower the weights by allowing the legs to return to the starting position.
- Inhale on the inward motion.

Summary

This section introduced a variety of lower-body exercises that can be performed safely by an experienced or novice weight lifter. One exercise should be chosen for each body part for an all-around toning program. To fulfill a specific objective, such as increasing the strength of the quadriceps, two or three quadriceps exercises are required. The choice of exercises depends on a number of factors, such as experience and personal goals. A spotter should be present during lifts that require great exertion.

There are a number of other exercises, not illustrated in this text, that also can be included in a training routine. The lifter must be cautious when attempting new exercises and attend to both personal safety and that of other exercisers in the vicinity. Before attempting an exercise observed in the gymnasium or read about in a magazine, the exerciser should consult a personal trainer regarding the correct techniques. An inexperienced weight lifter should master the correct techniques with the machine exercises before attempting free-weight exercises.

SUGGESTED READINGS

Baechle, T. R., ed. 1994. *Essentials of weight training and conditioning.* Champaign, IL: Human Kinetics

Baechle, T. R., and B.R. Groves. 1998. *Weight training: Steps to success.* Champaign, IL: Human Kinetics.

Fleck, S. J., and W. J. Kramer. 1997. *Designing resistance training programs.* Champaign, IL: Human Kinetics.

Garhammer, J. 1986. *Sports Illustrated strength training.* New York: Harper & Row.

Hesson, J. L. 1997. *Weight training for life.* Colorado: Morton.

Pearl, B. 1990. *Getting stronger: Weight training for men and women.* New York: Random House.

Stone, M., and H. Bryant. 1987. *Weight training: A scientific approach.* Minneapolis: Burgess International.

Design

After reading this section, the student will be able to do the following:

- Identify the preliminary and secondary considerations of weight training program design
- Identify internal and external factors that affect performance
- Design a program based on specific, individual goals
- Understand the benefits and drawbacks of using free weights and machines
- Discuss the factors affecting exercise selection

WEIGHT TRAINING DESIGN

This section of the text provides a brief discussion of some of the more common misconceptions of weight training and outlines the key components of program design. Essentially, the preliminary considerations are the foundation of the program and are those factors (personal goals, medical and exercise history, physical condition, time commitment, and accessibility) that guide its design. It is impossible to design an appropriate program before considering these preliminary factors. Secondary considerations build upon the foundations and shape the manner in which the program is to be performed. The secondary factors are the choice of exercises, type of resistance, exercise order, number of repetitions, number of sets, load assignment, volume, frequency, duration, and rest.

Misconceptions About Weight Training

Although the popularity of weight training has increased as a result of individuals realizing the benefits of health and fitness programs, numerous misconceptions concerning the effects of weight training on the body still exist. A common myth surrounding weight training is that it reduces muscular speed and causes clumsiness. Further myths suggest that weight training results in poor muscle flexibility, causes massive increases in muscular size, and impairs bodily coordination. These misconceptions result from the limited knowledge of individuals and incorrect guidance provided by some instructors who prescribe exercise programs. Contrary to these misinterpretations, a correctly designed and implemented weight training program can lead to increased flexibility and muscular speed and improved bodily coordination.

Preliminary Design Considerations

Personal Goals

goal *desired outcome to which the effort is directed*

A **goal** is the desired outcome to which effort is directed. An example of a weight training goal would be to improve strength in the biceps by increasing resistance by 15 pounds over a four-month period. The goals for participating in a weight training program differ from person to person, but popular goals include increasing strength, increasing muscle size, toning the muscles to enhance body shape, relieving stress, releasing pent-up anger and frustration, enhancing performance (sport and work related), and recovering from injury.

It is unlikely within a group of individuals, such as a fitness class or weight training class, that more than one or two people will require a similar weight training program. Therefore, different approaches to program design are required to achieve varied outcomes. For instance, to satisfy a goal of increasing muscular strength, the program should incorporate weights with relatively low repetitions, whereas a program designed to increase muscular endurance requires a higher number of repititions using less weight. A training program should, therefore, be individualized and reflect a person's ability and goals.

There are two important considerations when goal setting:

1. Goals should be measurable. For example, increase the weight on the biceps curl from 10 pounds to 12 pounds or perform 12 repetitions of each exercise. Goals that are not measurable serve little purpose and are difficult to adhere to.
2. Goals can be short- or long-term. Short-term goals usually represent objectives for the immediate future, such as increasing the size of the biceps by 1 inch in 4 weeks. Long-term goals usually require dedication over several months before they are realized. An example of a long-term goal is to reduce the percentage of body fat by 10 percent in 12 months. Ideally individuals will have both short- and long-term goals to motivate them with their programs.

Medical and Exercise History

It is a common practice of fitness facilities to require all participants to provide information regarding their medical and exercise history prior to exercising. This is ideal for the design of an appropriate program, but unfortunately, the information often is not used by the fitness staff for this purpose; often, it is only collected for insurance purposes and filed away indefinitely. Medical information not only helps in the design of a program, but ultimately can lead to greater exercise adherence and fulfillment of program goals. A brief medical history questionnaire can assist in the selection of exercises. For example, an individual who suffers from lower-back pain when lifting or digging may require exercises to strengthen the lower back and abdominal muscles. For an individual who indicates a history of blackouts when lifting heavy objects, it obviously would be unwise to design a program requiring the lifting of weights above the head. As an individual's safety is a primary objective of all fitness facilities, medical history questionnaires should be screened by medically trained individuals. A referral should be made to a physician if there are any doubts regarding the suitability of exercise for an individual.

Exercise history can be equally important in the program design. Previous weight training experiences, successes, or failures should guide the design. For example, if an individual has little or no previous weight training experience, the routine initially should be designed around weight machines, which are easier to use in comparison to free weights, because the individual need not be unnecessarily concerned with balance and coordination. Similarly, an individual with a number of years experience will be able to provide valuable and specific feedback of past experiences and can participate in the program design.

Physical Condition

Individuals exhibit a wide variety of physiques and physical activity habits. Body shape, age, gender, and physical maturity all affect the ability of an individual to successfully take part in a weight training program. Distinct anatomical differences between males and females, such as height, weight, muscle fiber size, and body composition also dictate to a certain degree the type of training that can be employed and the effect the training will have on the body. Generally, a male has a larger skeletal frame than a female, which can support a greater amount of muscle tissue and provide the ability to exert a greater force. Additionally, males usually have a greater proportion of lean body mass and muscle than females, which equates to an increased strength potential. Such physical differences are evident not only between males and females, but also between people of the same gender and between different cultures. For these anatomical reasons, a weight training program should be individualized and realistically designed to a person's physical attributes.

An additional limiting factor to performance is that of **genetics**, which relates to the antecedents of traits (for humans, the genetic antecedents are obviously the parents). Apparent genetic limitations are height, body structure, and to a certain extent, weight. Training only can develop the body within its physical attributions, some of which are genetic. All individuals can benefit from weight training, however, although some may realize larger gains in actual strength due to genetic factors.

genetics relates to causal antecedents, such as one's parents

Time Commitments

Commitments outside the weight room, such as work, family, and social obligations, determine the availability of time to schedule a weight training workout. Unfortunately, the latter is frequently the first activity to be discarded when work and social pressures increase. The predicted duration and frequency of the workout should be realistically reflected in the program design. A flexible program designed with consideration of an irregular working pattern would be ideally suited for a person who is constantly traveling for business purposes and is unable to workout regularly at a fitness center. A regimented program can be designed for an individual who is able to devote an hour each day to training.

Contingency planning is important to the continued success of a weight training program. Without prior planning, these program relapses can be the first stage of dropout from training. An example common to the majority of people is the disruption caused by a vacation when attending a fitness club is impractical or impossible. One method to avoid a relapse is to incorporate simple and quick exercises in the regular workout that can be performed anywhere and do not require equipment. Exercises such as push-ups and sit-ups can be performed without equipment, and exercises such as biceps curls and triceps kickbacks can be performed using household objects such as cans of food or a shopping bag weighted with books or shoes.

Accessibility

The accessibility to training is another factor to be considered in program design. For some individuals, membership to a health club or fitness center is not feasible due to financial constraints, and access to weight training equipment in a gymnasium is not always available. Even the purchase of relatively inexpensive personal weights such as barbells and dumbbells can be too costly for some individuals.

Accessibility also relates to the location of the weight training equipment in terms of distance and suitability. Most fitness facilities are situated in populated areas, which causes problems for individuals living several miles from them. Personal weight equipment designed and manufactured for the home is ideal as an introduction to weight training, but it has limited use for exercisers who require the versatility provided by an abundance of machines and free weights usually found in a well-equipped facility.

Secondary Considerations

The following factors are included to aid the reader in designing a rewarding weight training program and also to introduce some frequently used weight training terms. After reading this section, the importance of the preliminary factors in guiding the program will undoubtedly be recognized.

Choice of Exercises

concentric contraction in which the muscle shortens

isometric muscular contraction during which the length of the muscle remains unchanged

eccentric contraction in which the muscle exerts force as it lengthens

There are a number of important considerations when choosing the exercises that are best suited to achieve individuals goals. An understanding of the major types of muscle actions will assist in selecting the most appropriate exercises. There are five main muscle contractions: concentric, isometric, eccentric, isotonic, and isokinetic.

A **concentric** contraction is the shortening of a muscle that reduces the angle between a joint. An example of a concentric contraction is the shortening of the biceps muscle when performing a biceps curl, bringing the lower arm toward the upper arm (see figure 3.1). The use of concentric muscular contractions is commonplace in a fitness facility and can be performed with free weights and on the majority of weight training machines.

An **isometric** contraction, often referred to as a static contraction, is a muscular contraction where the length of the muscle remains unchanged. An example of isometric contraction is the contraction of the triceps and chest when performing a bench press exercise on a machine loaded beyond an individual's normal concentric contraction ability (see figure 3.2). This type of training method leads to substantial increases in isometric strength, but it is not commonly employed in fitness centers or for athletic training because it has little value apart from the specific isometric exercises. Two additional reasons for the limited use of isometric exercises are the unavailability of isometric machines and a lack of understanding of isometric exercises among some individuals who prescribe exercise programs. Another psychological reason is that isometric training provides the exerciser with few visible signs of muscular work in comparison to concentric contractions, and thus provides very little motivational feedback.

An **eccentric** contraction is the lengthening of a muscle as it works against resistance. During the downward phase of a biceps curl, the biceps lengthens and works against the resistance, while the triceps muscle lengthens in a relaxed state (see figure 3.3). There are machines available that provide resistance for both concentric and eccentric contractions during the same repetition. These are designed to increase the negative resistance above that of the concentric contraction so that the muscles are thoroughly worked during the eccentric

Figure 3.1

Concentric contraction of the biceps while performing a concentration curl.

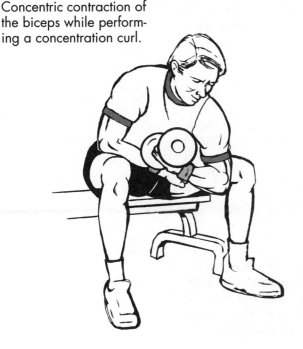

Figure 3.2 (on left)
Isometric contraction of
the triceps when pushing
against a wall.

Figure 3.3 (on right)
Eccentric contraction of
the biceps.

phase. During a concentric contraction, the negative resistance occurs during the eccentric phase of the exercise. For example, negative resistance of a biceps curl occurs when the weight is lowered after the curl.

An **isotonic** contraction is performed by keeping a constant muscular force throughout the contraction. Many of the movements referred to as isotonic in a fitness facility are by definition not isotonic in nature. An example of such an exercise is a bench press. Due to the structure of the pectoral muscles of the chest, the muscle is strongest at the top of the movement and weakest at the bottom. Thus, the force provided by the muscle is not constant because of strength changes. Manufacturers often design machines with cams (which vary the resistance across the range of movement) to offset the load when the muscle is weakest, thus ensuring that the muscle is worked maximally at all points in the range of motion.

isotonic contraction
performed by maintaining
a constant force

An **isokinetic** contraction is performed at a constant speed. Isokinetic machines limit the speed to ensure a constant velocity is maintained throughout the exercise. They are infrequently available in fitness facilities because they generally are more costly to purchase than concentric weight equipment. They are frequently available in clinics, however, where they are utilized for injury rehabilitation.

isokinetic contraction
performed at a constant
speed

Type of Resistance

Two basic types of weight training equipment are machines and free weights. Each has its own advantages and disadvantages and the decision of which is best suited for a training program should be based on the analysis of preliminary factors. The answer may lie in a combination of both modes of training.

Weight training machines come in many different forms and are manufactured by an increasing number of organizations. As technology improves, machines become more advanced and new exercises are developed. Weight machines can be multistationed, offering more than one exercise option, or single stationed, offering one specific exercise. Often a fitness center will offer both types of machines to its members. The benefits of weight machines include the following: they are safe for beginners because they are often limited to a fixed plane of motion; they do not require much balance and coordination; they allow exercises such as leg extensions and leg curls to be performed with greater ease than with free

weight machines
equipment that restricts
movement to ensure cor-
rect technique and safety.
Weights are stacked and
the resistance is altered
by moving a pin that sup-
ports the weights

weights; and they allow relatively heavy loads to be lifted safely without a spotter. The disadvantages of weight machines include the following: they restrict the range of movement outside that permitted by the machine; they are expensive, resulting in a limited number of machines in a facility; and they lack the versatility of free weights.

There are two types of free weights commonly available at a fitness facility—**dumbbells** and **barbells** (see figure 3.4). Dumbbells are handheld weights that can be used singularly or as a pair. Generally, dumbbells are of a fixed weight and can range from 1 to 200 pounds. As the name suggests, barbells are bars that hold weights at both ends. They come in different lengths and are sometimes shaped to improve the lifter's grip on the bar. Weights of equal mass are placed on each end of the bar to counterbalance it, and they are secured with safety collars to prevent them from falling off and causing injury. Large weights can be mounted on the bar and it is usually picked up with both hands. Advantages of free weights are that they are relatively inexpensive to purchase; they are portable; they allow exercises to be performed through a great range of motion; and they allow for versatility in the approach to the exercises. The drawbacks of using free weights are that they require training prior to beginning a program; they (heavy weights) require the supervision of a spotter; and they require more time to perform than machines. Lower-body exercises with free weights are rarely seen in a "fitness" center because they require experienced individuals to supervise and a large amount of space to be performed safely. These exercises, however, are frequently performed in a "strength" or "bodybuilding" gymnasium.

The following is a checklist of the important factors to consider when selecting exercises and equipment:

1. Classification of exercises: Exercises can be classified as **structural** or **body-part**. A structural exercise recruits a number of different muscles of the body to perform the exercise. An example of a structural exercise is a power clean; various muscles of the back, legs, and arms are recruited when a barbell is lifted from the ground to the upper chest and then racked (see figure 3.5a–3.5e). This type of exercise requires special training because of the high risk of injury. A body-part exercise attempts to isolate one specific muscle or muscle group. Leg extensions, for example, isolate the quadriceps muscle in the front of the leg. Structural and body-part exercises can be performed with free weights and machines.

2. Specificity of exercises: It is important that exercises are appropriate to the desired outcomes or goals of the program. The selected exercises should work the intended muscles. If, for example, individuals wish to increase the muscle

dumbbells handheld weights that can be used singularly or in a pair

barbells bars of varying length that hold weights at either end

structural exercise requires the use of a number of different muscles to perform the exercise

body-part exercise attempts to isolate one specific muscle or muscle group

Figure 3.4
Barbell and dumbbell.

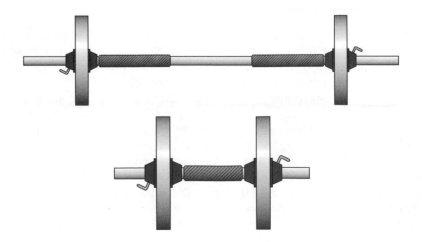

Figure 3.5
Power clean exercise.

size of the biceps, they should choose specific biceps exercises such as bicep curls, preacher curls, or concentration curls. Confusion often occurs when an exercise, such as a power clean, works more than one muscle group. Therefore, if time permits, it is advisable first to choose body-part exercises and then to incorporate additional structural exercises.

3. Muscle balance: Muscle balance refers to an equilibrium in strength or development between **agonists** and **antagonist** muscles (see figure 3.6a and 3.6b). Virtually all movements involve the action of more than one muscle. The muscle most directly involved in bringing about the movement is called the agonist and the muscle that slows or stops the movement is the antagonist. The biceps are the agonists and the triceps the antagonist for a biceps curl. The reverse is

agonist muscles that are primarily responsible for movement

antagonist muscles that oppose the movement of the agonists

Figure 3.6

Biceps curl showing the agonist and antagonist muscles.

a

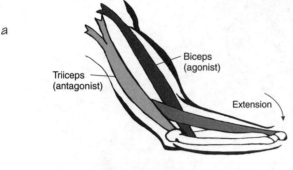

b

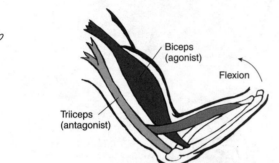

true for a triceps pushdown. Muscle balance is not only restricted to agonist and antagonist, but also can be a comparison between left and right and upper and lower body. Muscle balance is particularly important for bodybuilders who require definition of numerous upper and lower body muscles to satisfy the stringent marking of judges. The design of a total body exercise routine should include exercises for all the major muscle groups. An exercise for the biceps should be balanced with an exercise for the triceps, leg extension with leg curl, abdominal curl with back curl, and so forth.

4. Other factors such as time constraints and availability of equipment also affect the exercise selection.

Exercise Order

There are a number of conflicting theories in the literature as to the best order of exercises in a weight training program. Some people argue that the correct order is to work the major muscle groups first, followed by the small muscle groups. Others believe that a muscle group should be worked to exhaustion before moving on to the next.

Basically the order is determined by individual goals and the type and number of exercises selected. Due to individual differences, one of the ways to decide which order is appropriate is to experiment with the sequence until a suitable routine is found. A beginner who wishes to develop muscles all over the body, however, could begin by selecting one exercise for each of the major body parts. An example of this type of program is illustrated in table 3.1.

In addition to the exertion of a major group, the majority of body-part exercises require the assistance of other muscles when lifting a weight. For example, in a bench press, the triceps support the pectoral muscles. This is an important factor to consider when designing a program, particularly when recovery time is

TABLE 3.1	Example of a weight training program for a beginner wishing to tone all major body parts.	

EXERCISE ORDER	BODY PART	EXERCISE SELECTION (ALL MACHINES)
1	Chest (Pectoral)	Bench Press
2	Upper Back (Latissimus Dorsi)	Lat Pull-Down
3	Front of Upper Leg (Quadriceps)	Leg Extension
4	Back of Upper Leg (Hamstrings)	Leg Curl
5	Front of Upper arm (Biceps)	Concentration Curl
6	Back of Upper Arm (Triceps)	Triceps Pushdown
7	Midriff (Abdominal)	Abdominal Curl
8	Lower Back & Buttocks (Gluteus)	Back Raises
9	Back of Lower Leg (Gastrocnemius)	Calf Raises

of significance to the desired outcome. The order of exercises in table 3.1 allows adequate time for one body part to recover by moving to another region of the body (e.g., from the back to the legs). One factor to consider when designing this type of program (to tone all muscles) is to incorporate exercises that will yield muscular balance. An exercise of the agonist should be followed later in the program by an exercise of the antagonist. The number of repetitions and the quantity of sets are determined by the availability of time.

Number of Repetitions

Repetitions are the number of times an exercise movement is consecutively repeated. The number of repetitions performed is initially determined by the underlying objective of the program. Strength increases are usually accomplished by combining low repetitions (1–6) with heavy weights, whereas endurance increases are developed with higher repetitions (10–20) and light weights. Repetitions are often referred to in terms of **repetition maximum (RM)**. The RM is the maximal load that can be lifted for a certain number of repetitions. For example, an exerciser is said to have a leg extension capacity of 10 RM at 100 pounds.

repetition maximum (RM) maximal load that can be lifted a given number of times

One common procedure in designing a weight training program is to determine the **absolute strength** output of an individual with a test for 1 RM. To find the 1 RM, the exerciser begins by lifting a relatively heavy weight supervised by a spotter. Weights are progressively added until the exerciser cannot lift the load. The heaviest load lifted is referred to as the 1 RM. Rest periods between each attempt allow the exerciser to recover and the spotter to change the weight. Obviously, it is important to thoroughly warm up prior to attempting the 1 RM. After establishing the 1 RM for various body parts, a calculation can be made to set relative intensities. One training design uses a percentage of the 1 RM to establish a progressive increase in weight over 3 sets of the exercise. For example, the first set is at 50 percent of 1 RM, the second set at 55 percent, and the third set at 60 percent. Each set can be performed to exhaustion or limited to a certain number of repetitions.

absolute strength the maximal amount of force a muscle is able to sustain

Number of Sets

A **set** is a group of repetitions in one attempt of the same exercise. Typically a workout will consist of 2 more sets of each exercise, although the load and number of repetitions of each set may differ. Table 3.2 is an example of 3 sets of a leg extension exercise.

set group of repetitions performed in one attempt of the same exercise

Load Assignment

The **load** is the amount of weight per repetition. Usually the load is kept constant throughout the set, although a number of computerized machines adjust the load during the set according to the strength of the individual. The load should be considered along with the repetitions and sets and in association with the preliminary factors described earlier. Performing a 1 RM test will assist in the design of the program. Basically, a percentage of the 1 RM is utilized in each workout for a specific number of

load amount of weight lifted per repetition

TABLE 3.2	Example of 3 sets of leg extension exercises.	
Set 1	10 repetitions	80 lbs
Set 2	8 repetitions	90 lbs
Set 3	6 repetitions	100 lbs

repetitions and sets. Beginners should start with a light load and increase it. Adding too much weight early in the program can lead to injury of the muscles, bone, and connective tissue. It is generally regarded that strength training requires loads of 84–92 percent of 1 RM at 4–8 repetitions, and endurance training requires loads of 50–70 percent of 1 RM at 15 to 25 repetitions. Moderate improvements in strength and endurance can be achieved at loads that permit 6 to 12 repetitions.

Volume

volume *for one session the number of repetitions x sets x load*

The training **volume** for one session is the number of repetitions x sets x load. The weekly training volume is determined by summing the training volumes of each session in the week.

Frequency and Duration

frequency *number of times an exercise or workout is performed*

duration *amount of time spent on an exercise or workout*

The **frequency** is the number of times an exercise or workout is performed and the **duration** is the amount of time spent on an exercise or workout. Some of the factors that determine the frequency and duration are the availability of time, the goals of the program, and the health and physical condition of the individual.

Rest

rest *recovery time between sets of exercises and between sessions*

The **rest** period is the recovery time between sets of exercises and between sessions. The duration of rest between sessions is determined by the time it takes the body to replenish the energy used during the activity. Insufficient rest can have a detrimental effect on performance and can lead to injury, boredom in the training routine, and health problems. Appropriate rest is the most important factor in any form of athletic performance. The goals of the program affect the length of rest between sets, with strength training requiring longer rest (3 minutes) than endurance training (1 to 2 minutes). A general rule is to allow each muscle group to recuperate for 48 hours between sessions.

Summary

This section introduced the reader to the preliminary and secondary considerations of weight training program design. The primary objective of the design process is to develop a program that satisfies the aims and desires of the individual. In addition, factors such as medical and training history, availability of time and resources, and physical capability affect the design. Once a preliminary analysis is completed, a program can be created using the framework of secondary factors.

DESIGNING SPECIFIC WEIGHT TRAINING PROGRAMS

After reading this section, the students will be able to do the following:

- Understand the difference between muscle strength, muscle endurance, muscle power, muscle size, and muscle tone
- Determine the number of days per week needed to weight train
- Know the difference between core and auxiliary exercises
- Properly select core and auxiliary exercises to facilitate the desired outcomes
- Know the proper order of exercises to maximize each training session
- Know the proper number of sets, repetitions, and intensity for different types of weight training programs
- Know the proper rest needed between sets, exercises, and days of training

This unit provides an overview of the steps that should be taken when designing a personal weight training program. The first is to establish personal goals and needs, as detailed previously. Next, the individual must select the number of days on which he or she will train. This is related to the next two steps; determine the choice and order of exercises that should be performed. After the specific exercises and order are established, it is important to determine the appropriate sets, repetitions, and load that should be used. This step depends to a great degree on the individual's specific needs. The final stage is determining the rest period between sets, exercises, and workouts.

Personal Goals and Needs

The previous element discussed the role of choosing personal goals when beginning a weight training routine. These goals are the desired outcomes the individual wishes to attain, and they determine the specific components that need to be trained. Common components that individuals attempt to develop include muscular strength, muscular endurance, muscular power, muscle tone, and muscle size.

Muscular Strength

Muscular strength is the force a muscle can exert against a resistance in one maximal effort. For effort, an individual who can bench-press 200 pounds for a single repetition is said to possess more muscular strength than another individual who can bench-press 160 pounds for 6 repetitions. Muscular strength is important in several life style areas, including sport, manual labor, and everyday activities. Many weight training programs begin with a goal of increasing muscular strength because it is essential for other components, including power, hypertrophy, and tone.

Individuals beginning a weight training program should first concentrate on basic muscular strength. This initial strength-training phase aids in adaptation of the muscles: the neural and muscular systems learn to coordinate the movements associated with weight training. Recent research has suggested that initial gains in muscular strength for the first 8 weeks of a weight training program for an inexperienced individual are the result of gains neuromuscular adaptations. Therefore, lighter weights should be used at the beginning of a program to minimize the risk of injury.

muscular strength
amount of force a muscle can exert against a resistance in one maximal effort

Muscular Endurance

Muscular endurance is defined as the ability of a muscle to exert a submaximal force over a sustained period of time. Using the previous example of the two individuals performing a bench press, the individual who pressed 160 pounds for 6 repetitions possesses more muscular endurance than the person who presses 200 pounds for a single repetition. Individuals who train for muscular endurance experience some gains in muscular strength due to the adaptations of the nervous system referenced earlier. Sports such as wrestling and cross-country skiing require a great amount of muscular endurance, as do many recreational activities such as walking, swimming, and racket activities.

muscular endurance
ability of muscles to persist in exerting a force over a period of time

Muscular Power

Muscular power, defined as the product of the amount of force and distance over time, is the muscle's ability to release an explosive muscular force. The focus of muscular power is to move an amount of weight as quickly as possible. A defensive lineman in football, for example, must have a certain amount of power to move fast

muscular power *muscle's ability to release an explosive muscular force* and forcefully once the football has been snapped. Other sport performances, such as discus throwing or volleyball spiking, rely heavily on muscular power.

Muscle Size

Increases in muscle size (also referred to as *hypertrophy*) are the most physically visible results of a weight training program and are due to an increase in the size of the muscle fibers.

Muscle Tone

muscle tone muscle tissue which is firm, sound, and flexible

Muscle tone refers to muscle tissue being firm, sound, and flexible. While individuals train for muscle tone, it is difficult to measure progress since each person has different standards of when muscle tone is achieved. Beginning weight lifters should first work to increase muscular strength, endurance, or size since all these are quantifiable and lead to gains in muscle tone. Also, gains in muscle tone are the result of a combination of gains in muscular size and strength, as well as a decrease in the percentage of body fat. A program designed to increase muscle tone must also include cardiovascular training.

Number of Training Days

total-body workouts weight training program in which the lifter trains all the major muscle groups in one day

split workouts weight training program that emphasizes different muscle groups on different days of training

Once individuals have decided on the specific components they wish to train, careful consideration needs to be placed on the number of days that they train. There are several routines that incorporate anywhere from 3 to 6 days of training, each based on an individual's goals and time constraints. Examples of routines are 3 days per week **total-body workouts** and 4 to 6 days per week **split workouts**. It should be clarified that more is not always better. A person who wishes to optimize muscular strength can receive the same benefits from a 3-day-week routine as opposed to one of 6 days per week.

Total-Body Routines

Most individuals who are beginning a weight training program select a 3-day-per-week total-body routine. The person may train daily on a Monday-Wednesday-Friday or a Tuesday-Thursday-weekend schedule. During the training sessions, all the major muscle groups are worked. Advantages of a total-body workout include the following: the individual is only required to train 3 days per week; a day of rest between exercising allows the muscles to recover and replenish energy stores; and as the body is trained as a whole, several total body exercises such as the power clean and power snatch can be incorporated. However, there also are some disadvantages to this routine design: these routines generally result in longer training sessions; and the selection, order and intensity of the exercises need to be carefully chosen since the same muscle groups are being worked 3 times per week.

Split Routines

Split routines consist of training different muscle groups on different days. The best example of this is alternating between upper and lower body each session so that each muscle group is worked two times per week. Table 3.3 provides examples of whole and split routines. Many bodybuilders attempt a split routine in which they train 6 days per week. This is not recommended for novice weight lifters because it may lead to overtraining and psychological fatigue. Another type of split routine that should be avoided for the beginning lifter is that of working opposing muscle

TABLE 3.3	Sample routines.					
MON	**TUE**	**WED**	**THUR**	**FRI**	**SAT**	**SUN**
A. Whole Body	Rest	Whole Body	Rest	Whole Body	Rest	Rest
B. Upper Body	Lower Body	Rest	Upper Body	Lower Body	Rest	Rest
C. Upper Body	Lower Body	Upper Body	Lower Body	Upper Body	Lower Body	Rest

A is an example of a 3-day-per-week whole-body routine
B is an example of a 4-day-per-week split routine
C is an example of a 6-day-per-week split routine

groups on different days. An example of this would be to work the chest and biceps one day and the upper back and triceps the next. This type of routine leads to over-training of certain muscle groups, such as the shoulders that are used as synergist muscles in training all of the above muscle groups. As opposed to the whole-body regimen, the split routine has the advantage of shorter training sessions, which may be helpful for individuals with limited time to train; and each muscle group is only trained twice a week, allowing the body a greater recovery time and less chance for injuries due to overuse. A disadvantage of a split routine is that it requires the individual to train a minimum of 4 days per week and may limit the time available for other types of fitness training, such as cardiovascular exercise.

Choice of Exercises

The choice of exercises should be based on the experience, initial strength, and specific goals of the lifter. Young and inexperienced weight lifters should be supervised by an instructor or coach and either stay with simple exercises that move as few joints as possible or perform complex exercises that require movement of multiple joints (such as power cleans and snatches) using very light weights. Multiple and single-joint exercises are commonly referred to as **core exercises** and **auxiliary exercises**.

core exercises require several body joints and muscles to move during the lift

auxiliary exercises move only a single joint and few muscle groups

Core and Auxiliary Exercises

Core exercises are those that require several body joints and muscles to move during the lift. An example of this is the bench press which requires movement at both the shoulders and elbows and contraction of the musculature of the chest, shoulders, and upper arms. Core exercises are generally used when an individual wishes to develop strength, power, and size. These exercises also are beneficial as many muscles are working at the same time; muscle balance is maintained; and the time of the workout will be reduced. However, the beginning weight lifter should be advised that core exercises normally require muscular coordination and proper spotting. Table 3.4 lists some common core exercises.

Auxiliary exercises refer to those that only move a single joint and a few muscle groups. An example of this type of exercise is a biceps curl which requires the movement of the elbow and muscles of the upper arm and forearm. Table 3.5 lists examples of auxiliary exercises that are used to increase muscle tone (since each muscle can be isolated). One disadvantage of auxiliary exercises is that a routine consisting of several auxiliary exercises results in a lengthy training session.

It should be noted that a good weight training program consists of a combination of core and auxiliary exercises. The emphasis placed on each form of exercise should be manipulated to bring about the intended results.

TABLE 3.4	Core exercises.	
UPPER BODY	**LOWER BODY**	**WHOLE BODY**
Bench Press	Squats	Power Clean
Lat Pull-down	Leg Press	Power Snatch
Lat Row	Dead Lifts	
Military Press		

TABLE 3.5	Auxiliary exercises.	
UPPER BODY	**LOWER BODY**	**MIDSECTION**
Arm Curl	Leg Extension	Abdominal Crunch
Shoulder Shrugs	Leg Curl	Back Extension
Incline Press	Toe Raise	Oblique Crunch

Order of Exercises

The order in which a person performs exercises can enhance the benefit from each training session. Exercises generally are performed in the following order.

1. Core Exercises

Core exercises should be performed before auxiliary exercises. The core exercises require mental concentration and should be performed before an individual becomes fatigued. Performing the auxiliary exercises first will disrupt the balance of the muscles being worked. For example, if individuals first perform a leg extension to train the quadriceps, followed by a squat, they will be able to lift only as much weight in the squat as the tired quadriceps will allow. This inhibits the glutei and hamstrings from receiving a maximum workout from the squat exercise. Also, the highly skilled or explosive core lifts such as power cleans and snatches should be performed before slower core lifts such as the squat or dead lift. Table 3.6 shows an example emphasizing the performance of core exercises at the beginning of a routine.

2. Weakest Areas

Many people first train the weakest muscle groups of the body. Doing this gives the individual the psychological advantage of complete concentration during the exercises that are the most difficult for him or her to perform. Working the weaker areas first while rested results in greater gains for the muscle groups, which results in better muscle balance over time.

3. Rotating Areas

The order of exercises can vary from one session to the next. For example, during a 3-day-per-week whole-body routine, the lifter may perform upper-body exercises, lower-body exercises, and abdominal exercises on the first day. The next training

TABLE 3.6 Exercise order—core first.

1. Squat
2. Dead Lift
3. Leg Extension
4. Leg Curl
5. Toe Raises

TABLE 3.7 Exercise order—rotating emphasis.

DAY 1	DAY 2	DAY 3
1. Bench Press	Abdominals	Squats
2. Squats	Bench Press	Abdominals
3. Abdominals	Squats	Bench Press

day, abdominals may be trained first, followed by upper-body exercises, and then lower-body exercises. On the third day of training, the lower body should then be trained first, followed by the abdominals, and the upper body (see table 3.7). By rotating the emphasis placed on muscle groups at the beginning of the routine, the individual is able to work on each muscle group when the whole body is rested and the individual is able to concentrate.

4. Push–Pull Order

Exercises can be divided by the movement of the joint and are normally categorized as pushing or pulling exercises. The bench press is an example of a push exercise, while the lat pull-down (exercising the back) would be classified as a pull. Weight lifters often alternate between push and pull exercises. This can be of great advantage during split-day routines in which only a certain area of the body is being trained. An example of a push–pull order is given in table 3.8.

5. Upper- and Lower-Body Exercises

During a whole-body routine, it may be advantageous for the lifter to alternate between an upper- and lower-body exercise (see table 3.9). This will allow a group of muscles to recuperate while another group is being trained. As stated earlier, when choosing this order, it is best to perform the more complex lifts at the beginning of the routine.

Sets, Repetitions, and Intensity

To reiterate from the previous discussion, *repetitions* are the number of times a person performs an exercise without resting during one set. A person who performs 10 abdominal crunches without resting is said to have performed 10 repetitions. Repetitions are often abbreviated as "reps." A *set* is a completion of several reps performed in one attempt of the same exercise. A short rest period is usually taken between sets of an exercise. An individual who performs 10 reps of a biceps curl then takes a brief rest and repeats the activity is said to have performed 2 sets of 10 reps. When de-

TABLE 3.8	Exercise order—push–pull.
UPPER BODY	**LOWER BODY**
1. Bench Press (push)	Squat (push)
2. Lat Pull-down (pull)	Deadlift (pull)
3. Military Press (push)	Leg Extension (push)
4. Arm Curl (pull)	Leg Curl (pull)

TABLE 3.9	Exercise order—upper body/lower body.

1. Bench Press
2. Squats
3. Lat Pull-downs/Lat Rows
4. Leg Curls
5. Military Press
6. Toe Raises

intensity *amount of weight that is being used*

signing a weight training program, 2 sets of 10 reps is often abbreviated as 2 x 10, with the first number representing the number of sets and the last number representing the number of reps. **Intensity** refers to the amount of weight being used for each exercise and usually is classified as a percentage of a person's one repetition maximum (1 RM) for that specific exercise. It also can be categorized as low, moderate, or high, depending on the 1 RM percentage that is being used (see table 3.10).

However, it should be noted that an individual who uses this classification needs to constantly reevaluate his or her strength. For example, an individual who performs a bench press at a high intensity using 200 pounds one week may discover that weeks later, the 200-pound bench press is of low or moderate intensity. The sets, reps, and intensity of an exercise will vary depending on the individual goals and needs of the lifter. The following text explains the sets, reps, and intensities needed to achieve gains in muscular strength, endurance, power, size, and tone.

Muscular Strength

No single combination of sets and reps has been found to maximize gains in muscular strength. However, the majority of research suggests that the number of sets should be between 3 and 9 with 3 to 8 repetitions or 4 sets of 6 repetitions. Gains in muscular strength are normally achieved with a high intensity effort. Table 3.11 represents samples of sets and reps of core and auxiliary exercises for gains in muscular strength.

TABLE 3.10	Classifying intensity.
High	90–100% 1 RM
Moderate	80–90% 1 RM
Low	70–80% 1 RM

TABLE 3.11	Sets, reps, and intensity for muscular strength.	
SETS	REPS	INTENSITY
3–6	4–10	High (90–100% 1 RM)

Muscular Endurance

Muscular endurance requires a lifter to perform 2 to 4 sets for 10 to 20 reps. As stated earlier, many people who train for muscular endurance also see gains in strength. Because of this, the intensity of endurance training should be at a low to moderate level but still in the overload zone (see table 3.12). As the levels of intensity are lowered, there will be less gain in muscular strength.

Muscular Power

A power program involves fewer sets, repetitions and exercises with heavier loads and intensities (see table 3.13). Many power programs also will incorporate whole-body exercises such as power cleans and snatches.

Muscle Size

Muscle size or hypertrophy is defined as the enlargement of muscle fibers. Bodybuilders are individuals who train for gains in muscular hypertrophy. This type of training normally requires long sessions, as both the sets and reps increase (see table 3.14). Gains in hypertrophy are normally established at a low levels of intensity; however, experienced bodybuilders often incorporate periods of heavy training in order to increase total body thickness.

TABLE 3.12	Sets, reps, and intensity for muscular endurance and tone.	
SETS	REPS	INTENSITY
2–4	10–20	Low to Moderate (70–100% 1 RM)

TABLE 3.13	Sets, reps, and intensity for muscular power.	
SETS	REPS	INTENSITY
3–5	2–3	Very High (95–100%)

TABLE 3.14	Sets, reps, and intensity for hypertrophy.	
SETS	REPS	INTENSITY
3–10	8–12	Low (70–80% 1 RM)

Muscle Tone

Many people who wish to combine muscular strength, endurance, and size establish a *muscle tone* program. While muscle tone incorporates all three of the previous components, none of them is maximized. The sets, reps, and intensity for obtaining muscle tone are similar to those for muscular endurance. Individuals who wish to start a muscle-toning program should refer to the section on muscular endurance.

Rest Periods

The rest periods of a weight training routine are just as important as the actual time spent exercising. The rest period allows the muscles to repair damaged tissue and replenish needed energy reserves. Insufficient rest between sets, exercises, and workouts results in injuries due to overtraining and overuse.

Rest Between Sets

The amount of rest between sets differs on the type of training. Individuals training for muscular endurance and muscular strength need only 30 to 60 seconds and 90 to 180 seconds respectively between sets. Individuals who are training for gains in muscular power require 3 to 5 minutes rest between sets. Table 3.15 recaps the amount of rest needed between sets. It is important to rest no more than 5 minutes between sets as the muscles will begin to cool down, thereby increasing the risk of injury.

Rest Between Exercises

The amount of rest between exercises is dependent upon the number of days trained and order of exercises. In a total-body workout, for example, it is appropriate to immediately begin a lower-body exercise after one for the upper body if the lifter is alternating between upper- and lower-body exercises. However, when the intensity of training reaches high levels, 2 to 3 minutes between upper- and lower-body exercise is recommended. During a split routine, it is best to rest for 2 to 3 minutes between exercises since all exercises are for a specific area.

Rest Between Workouts

The rest period between workouts is probably the least understood and most neglected factor of a novice weight lifter. While muscle appears to increase in size during exercise, the actual growth and adaptations of muscles are taking place during the days of rest. When a muscle is stressed beyond its normal capacity, a certain amount of time is necessary for recovery. If this time is too short, the muscle

TABLE 3.15 Rest periods between sets.

Muscular Endurance	30–60 secs
Muscular Strength	3–5 min
Muscular Power	3–5 min
Hypertrophy	2–3 min
Toning	1–2 min

becomes fatigued and the amount of force it can exert is decreased. While the amount of recovery for a muscle differs from individual to individual, 48 to 72 hours between workouts is sufficient for the body to repair and replenish the muscle groups that were trained. However, individuals who are training at very high intensities may require longer rest periods.

Periodization

A recent trend in weight training, especially with athletes, is the use of **periodization** to optimize performance and prevent overtraining. Periodization refers to organizing training sessions into cycles that differ in objectives, tasks, and content. Within the periodization model, the **macrocycle** is the overall training period. For most individuals, the macrocycle refers to a year of training; however, it may also consist of several years for such individuals as Olympic athletes. The macrocycle is composed of several **mesocycles** that consist of many weeks or months of training. The mesocycle is generally composed of **microcycles** that represent periods of one week of training. Most mesocycles consist of a preparatory phase, a competitive phase, and a transitional phase. Figure 3.7 uses arbitrary units for volume and intensity to show how they change over an entire macrocycle.

Preparatory Phase

As its name states, the first phase of the mesocycle is used to prepare the individual for competition. This phase consists of hypertrophy/endurance, strength, and power periods. The hypertrophy/endurance period occurs during the off-season

periodization *model of training that organizes sessions into cycles that differ in objectives, tasks, and content*

macrocycle *overall training period in a periodization model*

mesocycle *one of several stages of training which make up a macrocycle*

microcycle *periods of one week of training which are part of a mesocycle*

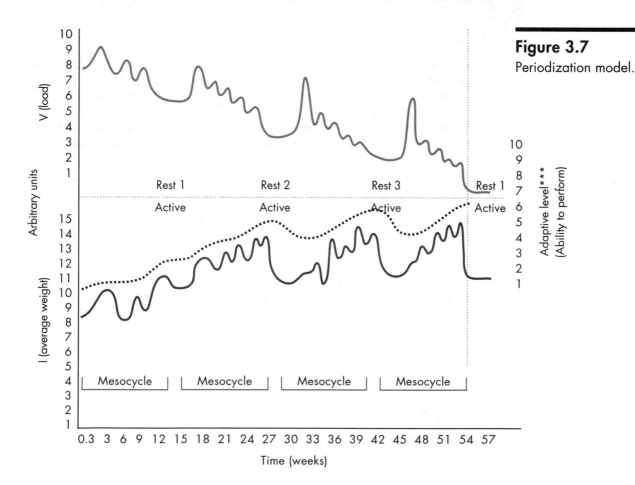

Figure 3.7
Periodization model.

prior to competition and is characterized by training that begins with low intensity and high volume. The main goal of this period is to increase both muscular endurance and size. A typical exercise would consist of 2 to 3 sets of 10 to 14 reps with an intensity of 70 percent 1 RM. As the preparatory phase progresses, exercises will decrease slightly in volume and increase in intensity. This strength period is the primary goal. An example of volume and intensity during the strength period would be 2 to 4 sets of 6 to 8 reps at 80–85 percent 1 RM. The last period of the preparatory phase is the power period during which the intensities continue to rise to levels of 90–95 percent 1 RM and exercise volume decreases to 3 to 5 sets of 2 to 4 reps. This period also is characterized by the implementation of explosive exercises such as power cleans and snatches.

Competitive Phase

Just prior to this phase, many individuals will add one or two microcycles of low volume and low intensity. This also is termed the "unloading period" that allows individuals to recover physically from the preparatory phase and mentally prepare themselves for the upcoming competitive season.

   During the competitive phase, the primary concern is to maintain muscular endurance and strength and allow individuals to achieve peak performance during the season. Depending on the length of the season, this phase may last from 4 to 20 weeks. While this phase is commonly characterized by high levels of volume and intensity, during longer competitive seasons, it is advantageous to manipulate the volume and intensity so as to not cause overtraining or injury. An example of volume and intensity for the competitive phase would be 1 to 2 sets of 3 to 4 reps at an intensity of 90 percent 1 RM.

Transitional Phase

The last phase of a mesocycle is the transitional period that immediately follows the competitive season and lasts from 3 to 8 weeks during the early off-season. During this phase, all activities should be of a low volume and intensity. Often, this is a time for many unstructured activities, such as cardiovascular training and participation in recreational sports. The purpose of this phase is to give the body time to repair both physically and mentally from the two previous phases of the mesocycle.

SUMMARY

The purpose of this unit was to introduce the steps to developing a personal weight training program. Before beginning a program, a person should evaluate his or her needs and goals. Depending upon whether the individual is seeking to increase strength, endurance, power, size, or tone, certain factors will be manipulated to bring about the desired outcomes. Besides individual needs, a person must decide the number of days he or she will train; the choice of exercises; the order of exercises; the sets, reps, and intensity of the exercises; and the rest periods.

Strategies and Special Considerations

After reading this section, the student will be able to do the following:

- Discuss the importance of applied sport psychology to performance enhancement
- Identify the major components of sport psychology
- Identify a number of psychological strategies to enhance performance
- Perform the psychological strategies to achieve goals

This section of the text discusses some of the psychological strategies that can be incorporated into a weight training program to enhance performance. The term *psychology* is defined and discussed in relation to its importance to weight training. The *optimal zone of functioning* also is defined and the psychological strategies to achieve this zone, such as concentration, visualization, effective goal setting, and arousal, anxiety and stress management, are discussed.

What Is Psychology?

The term **psychology** is defined as the science of behavior and mental processes. It is the study of how we learn, why we learn, our decision-making processes, and the ways that we mentally cope with daily situations. Sport psychology is a subdiscipline of the larger field of psychology and has its foundation in the principles of psychology applied to a sporting context.

Why Is Psychology Important to Weight Training?

It is common for coaches and athletes to attribute psychological processes to their successes in sport. Psychology is the means to realizing and accelerating the potential of an individual, and for many, it is the missing piece of the weight training and bodybuilding jigsaw puzzle. Psychological strategies have an extremely important role in performance enhancement, particularly at the highest levels of sport.

Weight training is not only a way to develop a better physique or improve fitness, but also to understand and develop the mental processes that control our lives

PSYCHOLOGICAL STRATEGIES FOR PERFORMANCE ENHANCEMENT

psychology *science of behavior and mental processes*

85

inside and outside the gymnasium. Weight training can lead to improvements in self-efficacy (exercise-specific self-confidence) and self-esteem and can help in the reduction of anxiety and stress. Additionally, weight training can accelerate learning and mental development. Using psychological skills to improve one's physique should be part of an approach that includes sports medicine, exercise physiology, and nutrition.

To highlight the importance of mental preparedness, consider the differences experienced across several exercise sessions. All athletes and exercisers experience sessions when they feel in tune with their bodies and minds, thereby enabling them to lift more weight, perform an extra set, and thoroughly enjoy the session. There are times, however, when a workout is an unenjoyable hassle, when one feels weak, uncoordinated, and tired. The difference from one session to another is mental and not caused by a significant decline in strength over a 24-hour period. These are times when it seems there is barely a connection between our actions and our thoughts. It is common knowledge that we accomplish more when we are mentally in tune with our bodies, so it is necessary to strive for this equilibrium every workout. This equilibrium is termed the **optimal zone of functioning.**

optimal zone of functioning *zone in which maximal results are achieved with a minimal amount of stress and strain*

Optimal Zone of Functioning

The optimal zone of functioning is that in which we achieve maximal results with a minimal amount of stress and strain. Similar to the optimal heart rate training zone for cardiovascular improvement, it is within the optimal zone of functioning that an individual attains his or her best mental results. Too much mental effort and intensity will exceed the optimal zone, and not enough will come up short of it. This is similar to training a muscle. Working a muscle too hard will take the body several days to recuperate, but if it isn't worked hard enough, no significant gains will be made. Each individual has a different optimal zone of functioning. One goal at the outset of a new training program should be to reach an optimal zone. More importantly, one must recall how the zone was acquired so that it will be possible to repeat it during the next workout. A psychological approach including concentration, visualization, goal setting, and anxiety and stress management will assist an individual in reaching the optimal zone of functioning.

Psychological Components

The following section of this text identifies some of the major components of sport psychology and suggests practical ways in which these components can be applied to improve performance.

Concentration

concentration *narrowing and sharpening mental focus to maximize physical movements*

Concentration is the narrowing and sharpening of one's mental focus to maximize physical movements. The aim of concentration is to sustain an intensity of mental effort to achieve a task.

Concentrating in a weight training environment is important for all individuals, and the appropriate degree of concentration is determined by individual differences in personality and program goals. For example, power lifters have to narrow their focus to sustain the intensity required to lift a heavy weight, whereas recreational weight trainers will probably not require such a focus. However, both the power lifter and the recreational lifter need to concentrate to perform an exercise correctly with good form and control. Without a certain degree of concentration, improvements are diminished and incorrect technique can lead to injury.

It is often difficult to remain focused when weight training. Gymnasiums are frequently the site of social gatherings that can lead to breaks in concentration and disruption of routine. Distractions such as taking long water breaks, observing the actions of others, waiting for equipment to become available, watching television in the gymnasium, and listening to music can all lead to lapses in concentration. Many of these distractions are out of an individual's control; however, the skill of concentration involves returning to the focused state as quickly as possible.

There are a number of techniques that can help keep the mind on the job at hand. Some people wear their own personal headphones, which have several benefits. Personal headphones (1) allow individuals to control their own music; (2) deter others from approaching for a discussion; and (3) help to prevent noise distractions from the televisions and other gymnasium music.

Some individuals focus their concentration by letting out yells and grunts as they start their set, while others find more success by closing their eyes and relaxing. Another excellent method of concentration and motivation is to train with a partner. Often it is easier to focus on training if a partner is also working within a similar regimen. Working with a partner also can create a competitive environment that leads to increases in the motivation and determination of an individual. Lifters should experiment with these techniques to find their most successful method. Once a technique is found to work, it should be adhered to.

The aim of concentration is to channel mental energies. Concentration techniques should begin during the warm-up, but prior to and during the main lifting routine, the aim should be to narrow the focus. If a distraction occurs during the session, an attempt should be made to immediately regain concentration. It is important to concentrate on certain exercises and the associated mental cues developed to maximize time and energy at the gymnasium.

Visualization

Visualization is the process of mentally planning, creating, evaluating, and solving problems. **Mental rehearsal** is a form of visualization used to create a mental picture or action prior to the performance of a skill. Visualization is a psychological technique that has been used with great success by high divers, gymnasts, and power lifters. Recently the importance of visualization as an extremely easy and effective training technique has emerged in other sports, such as baseball and basketball, as it helps to reduce nervousness, assists relaxation, and improves concentration.

Visualization is something we use in our everyday lives. We try to picture how we would look with a new haircut or how we would look behind the wheel of a new car, and when asked for directions, we commonly recall a route by drawing a mental picture. A number of research studies have suggested that combining mental rehearsal with an activity is more effective than doing either separately.

When are visualization techniques used? They are used to enhance performance prior to and during the workout and also to evaluate it at the end. While driving to the gymnasium, start to picture the exercises and the order in which they will be undertaken. If there are time restraints and only an hour can be spent at the gymnasium, try to conceptualize the length of time spent on each exercise. This will help establish realistic and attainable goals for the workout. When changing and preparing for the workout, start to think of the first exercise. Build a picture of the correct form, the breathing pattern, and the effort that will be required. Visualize success as the exercises are attempted. Picture achieving goals and accomplishing the final repetition. Recall how the muscles feel after a hard workout. Finally, after the workout, create and evaluate a picture of the previous workout. Recall successes and think of the strategies that will be employed to overcome the difficulties at the next session. In this instance, visualization is used as a form of feedback and reinforcement. Relaxation helps achieve a clear picture. Attempt to create a mental environment similar to daydreaming. After practicing this se-

visualization *process of mentally planning, creating, evaluating, and solving problems*

mental rehearsal *visualization technique used by an individual to practice a routine or action mentally, prior to performing*

quence, the benefits of mental imagery will be realized. Visualization is an excellent mechanism for realizing the benefits from a workout, is simple to learn, and produces results that are worth the effort.

Goal Setting

goal *desired outcome to which the effort is directed*

A **goal** is the desired outcome to which effort is directed. Goal setting is part of our everyday lives, from planning our workday to setting deadlines and organizing our time. Because effective goal setting can enhance performance, it is important that we carry over our goal setting to our workouts. Goal setting should be approached in an individualistic manner as each person is different and has his or her own reasons for participating in a weight training program.

Goals are crucial to the weight training program because they help to guide actions and provide a framework within which to proceed. Realistic goals are motivational and give exercisers an aim to work toward. Without goals, exercise can become boring and lead to erratic training with poor results.

Setting goals requires a needs assessment, first determining the reasons for lifting, and then outlining expectations. Research has confirmed that goal specificity enhances performance more so than general or "do-your-best" goals. Vague and general goals such as "to get bigger" and "to look better" are of little value because they are difficult to define and measure. Goals should be concrete, observable, and measurable. An example of a specific goal for an individual who wishes "to get big all over" would be to increase the dimension of the biceps by 1/2 and inch over a 3-month period. It also is important to state how the goal will be achieved. An increase in the size of the biceps can be achieved by working the muscles twice a week, for an hour each session, using three different biceps exercises. Goals can never be too specific, so the number of sets and repetitions to perform with each exercise also can be stated.

Setting realistic goals is important, for unrealistic goals can have a demotivational effect on the exerciser and prompt anxiety and distraction that impair perfor-

---

TABLE 4.1   Setting goals over time using a goal ladder.

Long-term Goal
Bench-press 150 lbs
Date: December 1st

Work 3 sets at 140 lbs. Repetitions to exhaustion
Date: August 16th–November 30th

Reduce the number of repetitions to 5 and work 3 sets at 130 lbs.
Date: August 15th

Workout 5 sets of bench press to exhaustion at 120 lbs.
Date: June 15th

Workout chest twice a week using 3 exercises for the chest: bench press, dumbbell chest flies, and incline chest press.
Date: April 1st–May 1st

Present performance: Bench-press 100 lbs.
Date: April 1st
Short-term Goals

mance. Research indicates that difficult but realistic goals enhance performance more than easy goals, which lead to a reduction in effort. A true sense of accomplishment can be derived from attaining a realistic, but difficult goal.

To have motivational value, individuals should set their own goals (rather than having a coach or fitness leader set the goals) and have a high degree of commitment to their achievement. A lack of commitment significantly reduces the effectiveness of goal-setting programs. Goals also can be sectioned into long-term, intermediate, and short-term. Research has suggested that short-term goals will lead to better performance than long-term goals, primarily because they offer the performer opportunities to assess success and correct effort levels, thereby enhancing motivation. Long-term goals are important because they provide an individual with direction for their efforts. It is important to establish several short-term goals that serve as intermediate steps in the achievement of a long-term goal. The formation of goals on a "goal ladder" is one method of goal setting. Table 4.1 illustrates how a ladder can be used to set long-term and short-term goals, with the bottom of the ladder representing performance at the present time and the top of the ladder representing the long-term goal.

Arousal, Anxiety, and Stress Management

The terms arousal, anxiety, and stress are frequently used interchangeably and in an inconsistent way, which often leads to confusion. **Arousal** is the physiological reaction of the body and mental activation that represents the intensity level of behavior. It ranges on a continuum from deep sleep to extreme excitement and can be measured through bodily responses such as heart rate and blood pressure. It can be assumed that during a weight lifting competition, a competitor will have a higher level of arousal than when performing routine exercises in the gymnasium. The intensity of arousal at any given time is determined by an individual's perception of the environment. The levels of arousal are closely associated with the optimal level of functioning. The aim is to become sufficiently aroused so that all concentration is focused on the training. Arousal that is too high or low will have a detrimental effect on performance.

It has been suggested that **anxiety** is the unpleasant emotional reaction that accompanies arousal. It is the feeling of nervousness and tension that is activated by arousal. Anxiety is believed to be subdivided into state and trait anxiety: **state anxiety** is defined as feelings of apprehension and tension that vary from moment to moment, whereas **trait anxiety** is part of a person's personality and is more constant and stable.

Stress can be viewed as the whole process by which we appraise and respond to events that threaten or challenge us. Some events can have a positive effect by arousing and motivating us to conquer problems. This type of positive stress is called "eustress." More commonly, we view stress as having a detrimental effect on our mental and physical well-being, termed "distress."

Although exercise and weight training generally are regarded as therapy for stress, they also can be stressful experiences in themselves. Working out in an environment with others present, or overtraining, can cause distress. Bodybuilders and power lifters often feel stressed when competitions approach and they are insufficiently prepared.

Relaxation techniques are particularly useful for reducing stress. Relaxing during a workout gives the mind and body the opportunity to adapt quickly to the stresses of training. Relaxing can result in a controlled pace that ensures a high level of mental quality throughout the whole session. Control of breathing during training is vitally important and can be an excellent technique to calm and relax nerves. Keeping a mental record of breathing patterns also provides a good indication of readiness for the next set. Music and visualization can take the mind away from the stressors.

arousal physical reaction of the body and mental activation that represents the intensity level of behavior

anxiety unpleasant emotional reaction that accompanies arousal

state anxiety feelings of apprehension and tension that vary from moment to moment

trait anxiety part of a person's personality that is more constant and stable than state anxiety

stress whole process by which we appraise and respond to events that threaten or challenge us

Summary

The purpose of this section was to introduce a number of psychological techniques that can enhance performance and help individuals reach an optimal zone of functioning. Techniques such as visualization and concentration help lifters attain a high level of performance by "tuning in" the body with the mind.

SUBSTANCES USED TO ENHANCE PERFORMANCE

After reading this section, the student will be able to do the following:

- Know the positive and negative side effects of pharmacological agents
- Know the effects of anabolic steroids on the body
- Understand the role of human growth hormone in the development of muscle and bone
- Know the dangers associated with blood doping
- Understand the proper use of nutritional supplements

ergogenic aids substances or phenomena that are believed to improve an individual's performance

This section of the text focuses on the agents believed to enhance performance, the way the body adapts to them, and the side effects that may result from their intake. Performance-enhancing agents are referred to as **ergogenic aids,** which generally are placed into four categories: pharmacological agents, hormonal agents, physiological agents, and nutritional supplements. Pharmacological agents are common drugs including alcohol, amphetamines, and caffeine. Several types of naturally occurring hormones often are taken in excessive quantities in an attempt to boost the results of training. The most common of these are anabolic steroids and human growth hormones. Physiological agents, such as blood doping, are now being used by athletes. These agents occur naturally in the body but are taken in excess to try to increase performance. The fourth category is over-the-counter nutritional supplements consisting of amino acids, vitamins, and minerals. Several amateur and professional organizations have published lists of illegal performance-enhancing aids, some of which are included in table 4.2.

Pharmacological Agents

pharmacological agents agents that may be added in excess to the body in an attempt to increase its function in physical activity

Pharmacological agents that are proposed to have ergogenic effects include alcohol, amphetamines, and caffeine.

TABLE 4.2   Agents used to enhance performance.

Pharmacological Agents	Alcohol
	Amphetamines
	Caffeine
Hormones	Anabolic Steroids
	Human Growth Hormone
Physiological Agents	Blood Doping
Nutritional Substances	Vitamins
	Minerals
	Trace Elements
	Amino Acids
	Herbs

Alcohol

Some athletes use alcohol for its proposed psychological effects. Claims have been made that it calms nerves, reduces inhibitions, and makes athletes alert. Recent research has shown, however, that alcohol has a detrimental effect on several psychological and physiological components of performance. It has been reported that alcohol can inhibit reaction time, movement time, speed, coordination, and information processing.

Many people have viewed alcohol as a good source of carbohydrates. However, it also is classified as an antinutrient because it interferes with the metabolism of other important nutrients. Another risk of alcohol in terms of performance is a decreased sensation of the central nervous system, which in turn can lead to a decrease in pain sensation. Participants must realize that pain is an indicator of an injury, and further participation while injured may increase the severity of the injury. Alcohol reduces the release of an antidiuretic hormone (ADH), causing the body to increase water excretion into the urine. This leads to a decrease in blood pressure and a risk of dehydration (figure 4.1), which is especially serious when physical performance is taking place in a hot environment. Alcohol also has detrimental effects during cold weather: alcohol causes blood vessels in the skin to dilate, which can result in a loss of body heat and possible **hypothermia.**

hypothermia *dangerously low body temperature*

Figure 4.1
Effects of alcohol: decreased blood pressure and dehydration.

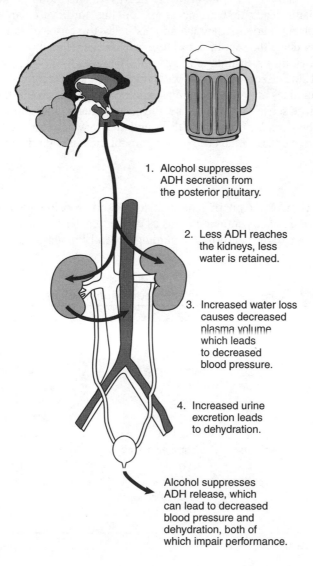

1. Alcohol suppresses ADH secretion from the posterior pituitary.

2. Less ADH reaches the kidneys, less water is retained.

3. Increased water loss causes decreased plasma volume which leads to decreased blood pressure.

4. Increased urine excretion leads to dehydration.

Alcohol suppresses ADH release, which can lead to decreased blood pressure and dehydration, both of which impair performance.

Amphetamines

amphetamines sub-
stances that work to
increase the stimulation
of the central nervous
system

Amphetamines are substances that work to increase the stimulation of the central nervous system and have been used in clinically controlled weight-loss studies as appetite suppressants. The first documented use of amphetamines as ergogenic aids can be traced back to World War II where they were used by army troops to combat fatigue and increase endurance. Soon after, these stimulants became associated with athletic performance.

Amphetamines are believed to aid performance by helping athletes run faster, throw farther, jump higher, and delay fatigue and exhaustion. As is typical with most ergogenic aids, the findings of studies concerning the effects of amphetamines have generated mixed results. People who have been under the influence of amphetamines and other similar stimulants are reported to have decreased sense of fatigue, increased blood pressure, increased heart rate, increased blood flow to the skeletal muscles, and increased muscle tension. Some of the more controlled and reliable studies, however, have shown that amphetamines increase several other aspects of athletic performance, including speed, power, endurance, concentration, and fine motor coordination.

While amphetamines have been shown to increase athletic performance, the use of these drugs is extremely dangerous, and several deaths have been attributed to excessive usage. The elevation of the heart rate and blood pressure caused by these stimulants leads to extreme stress on the cardiovascular system. While claims have been made that amphetamines delay the onset of fatigue, it is likely that they only delay the sensation of fatigue. This causes the body to be pushed beyond its normal limits, leading to irrevocable damage. Table 4.3 shows some of the documented side effects associated with amphetamine usage.

Amphetamines also can become psychologically addictive to the user because of the energized sensations they cause. Physical addiction and an individual's tolerance to amphetamines also build with extended use, which leads to the need for increasingly large doses of the drug to bring about the desired effects.

Caffeine

Caffeine is considered a pharmacological agent and probably the most widely used drug. It is found in such common items as coffee, tea, soft drinks, a wide variety of foods, and many common drugs, including several brands of aspirin. Caffeine is

TABLE 4.3 Acute and chronic effects of amphetamines.

ACUTE, MILD	ACUTE, SEVERE	CHRONIC
Restlessness	Confusion	Addiction
Dizziness	Assaultiveness	Weight loss
Tremor	Delirium	Psychosis
Irritability	Paranoia	Paranoid delusions
Insomnia	Hallucinations	Dyskinesia
Euphoria	Convulsions	Compulsive, stereotypic,
Uncontrolled movements	Cerebral hemorrhage	repetitive behavior
Headaches	Angina	Vasculitis
Palpitations	Heart failure	Neuropathy
Anorexia	Circulatory collapse	
Vomiting		

Adapted from Wadler & Hainline (1989).

TABLE 4.4 Caffeine content in foods and medication.*	
SUBSTANCE	**CAFFEINE (MG)**
Standard dose Prolamine	280
Standard dose Dexatrim, Dietac	200
Standard dose No Doz, Vivarin	100–200
6 oz automatic drip coffee	181
6 oz automatic perk coffee	125
Standard dose of some aspirin products (see labels)	30–128
6 oz hot tea (strong)	65–107
6 oz iced tea	70–75
6 oz instant coffee	54–75
12 oz cola beverages	32–65
12 oz Mountain Dew	54
12 oz Mello Yellow	51
8 oz chocolate milk	48
2 oz chocolate candy	45
1 oz baking chocolate	45

*Recommended caffeine intake is less than 250 mg per day.
Adapted from Tribole (1991).

considered a stimulant, and its effects are similar to those described in the discussion of amphetamines. Table 4.4 shows the caffeine content of several popular foods and medications.

The ergogenic effects of caffeine are probably the most documented of any of the pharmacological agents. Numerous studies have found caffeine to aid performance by increasing alertness, increasing concentration, elevating moods, decreasing and delaying fatigue, and decreasing reaction time. Alternatively, caffeine has been noted to have detrimental effects on performance in people who are not accustomed to using it or are sensitive to it. People who consume high doses may experience nervousness, restlessness, insomnia, and tremors. Caffeine is an addictive drug, and those who suddenly discontinue its use may experience headache, fatigue, irritability, and gastrointestinal distress. Finally, it must be stressed that caffeine acts as a diuretic, which increases an individual's risk of dehydration and heat-related illness.

Hormonal Agents

Hormonal agents are naturally occurring hormones believed to benefit the performance of physical activities. While these are naturally occurring, hormonal agents taken in excess of what the body produces can have irreversible side effects that could lead to death. Most studies in the scientific field of hormonal agents and performance have dealt with anabolic steroids and human growth hormones, which are the two most often used. These agents, subsequently, have been banned in nearly every sport and by athletic organizations at all levels around the world.

Anabolic Steroids

Similar to male sex hormones are **anabolic steroids,** whose building properties increase the growth of muscle and bone tissue. The intake of anabolic steroids increases fat-free mass and strength. An athlete who depends on muscle size and strength thus finds it very tempting to use steroids. Claims have been made that

hormonal agents naturally occurring hormones believed to benefit the performance of physical activities

anabolic steroids hormones that are similar to male sex hormones. The anabolic or building properties of these hormones increase the growth of muscle and bone tissue

anabolic steroids increase endurance and allow a fast recovery from exhausting bouts of exercise, which has even led some endurance athletes to use anabolic steroids to boost performance.

Few controlled studies have been published on the side effects of steroids on physical performance. One of the problems surrounding such studies is the inability to observe what goes on outside the laboratory. Also, the number and size of the doses claimed to be used by athletes varies. Figure 4.2 shows the side effects of anabolic steroid use over a 6-week period where significant increases in body mass, fat-free mass, muscle size, and leg strength were produced. Controlled studies have shown that anabolic steroids have little or no effect on cardiovascular endurance and recovery from training.

While anabolic steroids have been shown to increase muscle size and strength, their use is illegal in athletic events. Federal laws place restrictions on how and for what reasons anabolic steroids can be prescribed. Similarly, the majority of athletes believe that it is unfair to have to perform against athletes who use anabolic steroids to aid their performance. Several national and international organizations have published papers stating their position on anabolic steroid usage. Table 4.5 shows the harmful and irreversible effects of anabolic steroids on males and females.

Human Growth Hormones

human growth hormone
naturally occurring hormone that aids in building muscle

The most recent hormonal agent to be banned from athletic competition is a **human growth hormone (hGH)** secreted by the pituitary gland and regularly used in the medical treatment of dwarfism. Prior to the introduction of genetically engineered hGH in the mid-1980s, its availability was extremely limited. At the inception of widespread manufacturing of hGH, however, athletes and coaches began to delve into its capabilities for aiding and improving performance.

Figure 4.2

Effects of anabolic steroids on body mass, fat-free mass, muscle size, and strength.

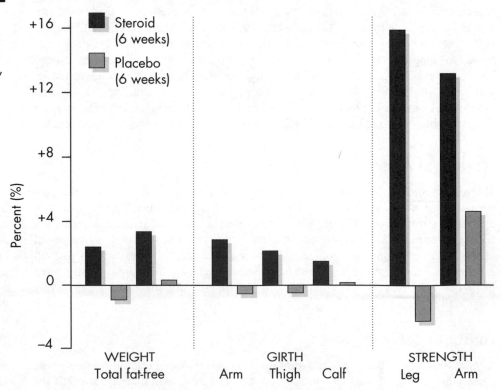

Percent of changes in body size, body composition, and strength, when using anabolioc steroids and a placebo. Adapted from Hervy et al. (1981).

TABLE 4.5	Side effects of anabolic steroid usage.
MALE	**FEMALE**
Decreased testicular size	Disruption of menstrual cycle
Reduced sperm count	Decreased breast size
Enlargement of the breasts	Deepening of the voice
Liver damage	Excess facial hair growth
Cardiomyopathy (diseased heart muscle)	Liver damage
Low level of HDL (good) cholesterol	Cardiomyopathy (diseased heart muscle)
Aggressive behavior	Low level of HDL (good) cholesterol
	Aggressive behavior

The ergogenic benefits of hGH include stimulation of protein synthesis in the skeletal muscle; stimulation of bone growth if the bones have not yet been fused; increase in lipolysis, which leads to a decrease in body fat; increase in blood glucose levels; and enhanced healing of musculoskeletal injuries. Since the use of hGH as an illegal ergogenic aid is fairly recent, limited research is available on its effects. However, studies have shown hGH to increase fat-free body mass, total body water, and protein synthesis.

Similar to anabolic steroids, usage of hGH leads to severe side effects, one of which is **acromegaly.** This is a debilitating disorder that causes bones to thicken, in turn broadening the hands, face, and feet. Acromegaly also causes the thickening of the skin and soft tissue growth. Other side effects of hGH usage include enlargement of internal organs, muscle and joint weakness, heart disease, glucose intolerance, diabetes, and hypertension.

Physiological Agents

The main reason for using **physiological agents** as ergogenic aids is to improve the body's physiological response during exercise. Normally an athlete will add a naturally occurring agent into the body to aid performance, as it is believed that if a normal level of a substance aids the body, then larger doses will lead to even greater benefits. As with the use of hormonal agents, the physiological agents are seen as unethical and immoral and have been banned from most competitive sports. The most widely known and researched physiological agent is **blood doping,** which refers to increasing an individual's total volume of red blood cells (used by the body as carriers of oxygen). Doping often is performed by a transfusion of the individual's own previously donated blood or a donation from someone with the same blood type. Theoretically, if more red blood cells are present, more oxygen will be available for the body to use and endurance levels will dramatically increase. While blood doping may not directly affect the performance of resistance weight training, due to the severity of its side effects, it should be included in this discussion of ergogenic aids.

Blood doping has been shown, in optimal conditions, to increase the body's overall aerobic capacity. For this to occur, there must be a minimum of 900 ml of blood transfused; there must be a minimum of 5 to 6 weeks between withdrawal and reinfusion; and the blood must be frozen during storage.

Along with the ergogenic benefits of blood doping come possibly deadly side effects. The addition of red blood cells into the body can overload the cardiovascular system, causing the blood to become extremely viscous and possibly resulting

acromegaly *debilitating disorder that causes bones to thicken, in turn broadening the hands, face, and feet. Also causes a thickening of the skin and soft tissue growth*

physiological agents *substances that are naturally produced by the body and are used in excess in an attempt to increase physical activity*

blood doping *increasing an individual's total volume of red blood cells*

in blood clots and heart failure. Several other complications can occur when another donor's mismatched blood is reinfused into the athlete, leading to allergic reactions chills, fever, or nausea—in addition to greater risk of exposure to hepatitis and the HIV virus.

Nutritional Supplements

Nearly every athlete has been exposed to vitamins, minerals, proteins, amino acids, and exotic herbs that claim to possess bodybuilding and fat-burning properties. Most of these claims are based on unproved theories from undocumented sources. While decreases in physical performance have been associated with deficiencies in vitamins and minerals, especially the B vitamin, it should not be assumed that increased vitamin dosage will increase athletic performance. False claims also have been made that the body undergoes a mass depletion of vitamins and minerals during physical activity. The majority of Americans already obtain the recommended daily allowance of vitamins and mineral in a normal healthy diet, and doses over this amount may be toxic to the body and cause harmful side effects.

trace elements naturally occurring elements that are needed by the body in small quantities

Two **trace elements** (naturally occurring substances that the body needs in small quantities) that purportedly increase performance are **chromium** and **vanadium.** Both these elements are created naturally in the body and are used to regulate how the body uses energy. The former, usually sold under the name of chromium picolinate, is believed to be involved in the regulation of glucose. Claims have been made that it enhances insulin action and improves muscle glycogen stores, which aids in increasing lean mass and decreasing body fat. However, few controlled studies have been able to support these claims when excess chromium is consumed. Vanadyl sulfate, the most commonly available form of vanadium, has not been shown to have any ergogenic effects, and several researchers have found excessive amounts of vanadium to be highly toxic to the body. Both these trace elements should be used with the utmost caution.

chromium trace element used in the regulation of glucose that has also been claimed to enhance performance

vanadium trace element that has been claimed to have ergogenic effects

Just as high doses of vitamins and minerals have been said to aid performance, so have high doses of **amino acids** and **proteins.** Amino acids are the building blocks of skeletal muscle; therefore, an increase in amino acids is thought to increase skeletal muscle growth. However, out of 22 amino acids, 12 are considered nonessential because the body is able to naturally synthesize them in adequate quantities. Of the nine essential amino acids, adequate quantities can be obtained through a proper diet, though studies have shown that more than normal intake is needed when weight training.

amino acids building blocks for skeletal muscle

proteins complex molecules that are responsible for body growth, maintenance and repair, and energy production

Many herbs and plants also have been claimed to have ergogenic effects on performance. Of these, the more popular include ginseng, bee pollen, tree bark, and shark cartilage; however, reputable research is lacking on the effects of these substances.

Summary

nutritional supplements nutrient that claims to possess bodybuilding or fat-burning properties

Many agents claim to enhance performance and can be categorized as pharmacological, hormonal, or physiological agents, or as **nutritional supplements.** The majority of these substances may cause harmful and permanent side effects, which has led most athletic organizations to set guidelines as to which ergogenic aids are illegal. Nutrients such as vitamins, minerals, and amino acids are consumed under the pretense that large doses will increase muscular growth and aid in performance. However, little research is available to substantiate this claim.

After reading this section, the student should be able to do the following:

- Discuss some of the misconceptions of weight training for prepubescent children, pregnant women, elderly persons, and individuals who are physically or mentally disabled
- Apply knowledge to weight training design to develop programs for individuals from these special groups
- Identify the distinct requirements of individuals from these groups

This section of the text provides a discussion of some of the misconceptions that surround weight lifting by prepubescent children, pregnant women, elderly persons, physically and mentally disabled individuals in addition to injury rehabilitation and considerations that should be included in the design of programs for these groups. Illustrations of exercises suitable for children also are provided.

Weight Training with Prepubescent Children

Exercise, in particular cardiovascular exercise, is popularly viewed as having an influence on the growth and physical fitness of children. However, weight training by prepubescent children has been a controversial subject for many years because it was commonly thought to be dangerous and ineffective. These beliefs are antecedents of misconceptions that resistance training can lead to deformity, spinal injury, and stunted growth. To the contrary, however, recent research has found that children can safely make significant gains in strength following a weight training program. A number of health organizations in the United States have found that prepubescent children can derive such benefits as increased muscular strength and endurance from well-designed and supervised weight training programs. Scientific studies also have found that many of the physical capacities of the mature adult depend largely on preparation that occurred during the early years of growth. It is apparent, therefore, that weight training can not only lead to improvements in muscular strength, but can also limit the risks of injury and enhance athletic performance.

Weight training and gymnasium-based exercise are becoming popular within the public school curriculum. Educators now are aware of the role that exercise plays in the reduction of cardiovascular disease, cancer, and hypertension and of the improvements in fitness and general health that result from exercise.

As with the adult population, the risk of injuries is greatly reduced with children who receive proper instruction and supervision in a thoughtfully designed program. Injuries are caused by incorrect technique and when undue physical and psychological demands are placed on children. It is vitally important, therefore, that realistic goals are set to avoid these demands. Each child is different in his or her physical and mental makeup, which should be reflected in individual program goals. One of the major problems with weight training programs is that the majority are designed for a group and not for individual children. A needs analysis that includes a review of a subject's past experiences, medical history, and programmatic goals is a good starting point in program design.

The principles of weight training for adults also should be applied in the design of programs for children. These principles include a 10 to 15 minute warm-up and stretch prior to training, and a 10 to 15 minute cooldown period. A weight training program for children should start with exercises that use their bodies' own resistance (see figures 4.3–4.18). Conditioning the muscles in a slow and deliberate manner helps avoid the risk of injury that would result from starting directly on weights. In addition, the majority of weight training equipment is designed for adults and not for children. The child must have the ability to perform an exercise

Figure 4.3
Bent-knee sit-up: starting position.

Figure 4.4
Bent-knee sit-up: upward motion.

Figure 4.5 (on left)
Assisted behind-the-neck pull-up: starting position.

Figure 4.6 (on right)
Assisted behind-the-neck pull-up: upward motion.

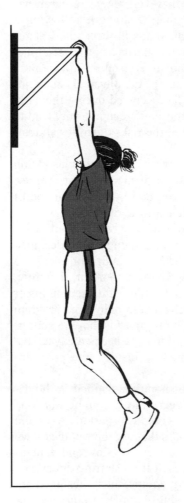

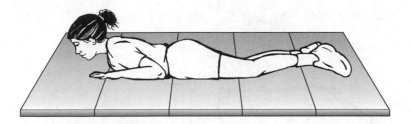

Figure 4.7
Lower-back raise: starting position.

Figure 4.8
Lower-back raise: upward motion.

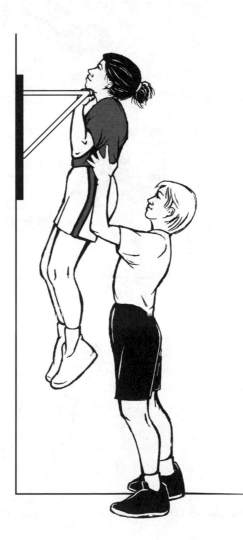

Figure 4.9 (on left)
Assisted chin-up: starting position.

Figure 4.10 (on right)
Assisted chin-up: upward motion.

Figure 4.11 (on left)
Triceps dip: starting
position.

Figure 4.12 (on right)
Triceps dip: upward
motion.

Figure 4.13
Bent-knee sit-up: starting
position.

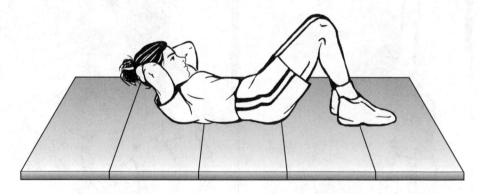

Figure 4.14
Bent-knee sit-up: upward
motion.

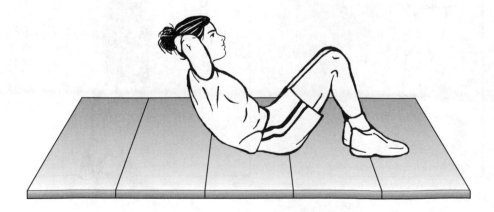

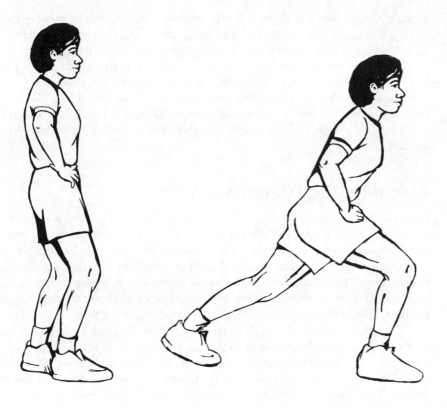

Figure 4.15 (on left)
Lunge: starting position.

Figure 4.16 (on right)
Lunge: forward motion.

Figure 4.17 (on left)
Standing calf raise:
starting position.

Figure 4.18 (on right)
Standing calf raise:
forward motion.

correctly; therefore, it is important to determine if the child is of suitable size to fit the equipment. In the event of a child being too small for weight machines, a supervised body resistance and free weight program is more appropriate.

Preparing the weights and determining the number of sets and repetitions can be a problem. Basically, children require a lighter resistance and a greater number of repetitions (10 to 20) than adults. Emphasis should be placed on improving quickness, speed, endurance, coordination, and flexibility because these are the basic elements for a healthy lifestyle and contributing factors for future sport success.

Weight Training During Pregnancy

Information is limited regarding weight training during pregnancy, and that which is available is often inaccurate. Similar to the case with children, there are many misconceptions surrounding weight training during pregnancy. It has been suggested that weight training can lead to premature birth, problems with the birth, and damage to the baby. These statements cause many women to be apprehensive and understandably steer them away from exercise. Some research, however, suggests alternatively that weight training during pregnancy is safe for the mother and the fetus.

Women with strong muscles experience less discomfort during pregnancy, enabling them to tolerate a heavy body and a change in its center of gravity. Physiological changes during pregnancy limit the ability as well as the desire to exercise. The appropriate level of training depends on the condition of the woman prior to the pregnancy. Ideally, for a subject with a good level of endurance and strength, the emphasis of the program should be on maintenance. Increases in strength are extremely difficult while the fetus develops. Special areas on which to focus are the leg, back, and pelvic muscles that are required to carry the weight of the baby.

Caution must be taken as pregnant women are at greater risk of ligament and soft-tissue injury than nonpregnant women. Heavy weights should be avoided, but light weights (dumbbells 1 to 5 lbs.) do not cause a problem. The best exercises are those that work one muscle group at a time, as structural exercises that recruit a number of muscles can be potentially dangerous. Weight machines are more appropriate than free weights because they restrict movement and are safer to use. It must be stressed, once again, that each woman should be prescribed a specific and individualized program after careful review of previous medical and exercise history.

Weight Training and Elderly Persons

Recent research has focused extensively on the effects of exercise on the aging process. After the age of thirty, there is a deterioration in most physical functions, which is due in part to changes in lifestyle, diet, and physical activity. The basic findings of the research is that exercise and weight training appear to inhibit the deterioration associated with aging by increasing muscular strength and endurance. Individuals up to ninety years of age are able to increase their muscular strength and fat-free mass through resistance training. Frail, older individuals have greatly reduced muscle mass and strength and face diseases such as osteoporosis and arthritis that predispose them to falls and impaired mobility. Incidentally, statistics show that injury due to falls is a leading cause of morbidity and mortality in the elderly population, with more persons aged eighty-five and older likely to die from falls than heart disease. Osteoporosis and arthritis have been found to be positively affected by regular weight training. Weight training not only strengthens muscle, but also increases the thickness of bones and produces an increase in lubrication around joints. Without weight bearing or weight lifting exercise, there is a rapid loss of bone density, but research suggests that individuals who do not regularly exercise can increase their bone density by becoming more physically active.

An increase in physical activity not only reduces the risk of falling, but also increases the ability to meet daily physical challenges, thereby helping individuals to maintain their independence. When older individuals can continue to be self-sufficient and mobile, their dependence on others and the chances of institutionalization are greatly reduced. As with other segments of the population, the elderly show improvement in mental status and cardiovascular function as a result of weight training interventions.

Although there seem to be fewer risks attributed to weight training in older populations than previously thought, there are risks worthy of mention. First, there is an increased risk of sustaining muscular and ligament injuries such as sprains and tears during training. Second, blood pressure rises considerably during a lift, which can be extremely dangerous for individuals receiving treatment for hypertension (high blood pressure). Increases in pressure, often resulting from improper breathing or incorrect lifting technique, can be considerably reduced through guidance and supervision.

There are certain procedures that can be followed to decrease risks. The duration of the weight lifting session can be reduced and can consist of dynamic strengthening exercises rather than isometric strengthening. The weights should be lifted through the entire range of motion in a slow and controlled manner, and bouncing and jerky movements must be eradicated. Prior to weight training, it is vital that the exercisers warm up and stretch correctly, and that after exercise, they cool down and stretch.

Weight Training with Individuals Who Are Physically or Mentally Disabled

There are several important considerations when prescribing weight training programs for physically disabled individuals. First, physically disabled individuals require more time to prepare for exercise than nondisabled individuals. Extra time must be allocated in the program design for getting in and out of the machines and adjusting the machines and spotting. Third, wheelchair exercisers require room to maneuver their chairs into position. And fourth, these exercisers are restricted physically by the availability of equipment that will allow for their handicap.

One particular form of physical disability is neuromuscular disorder (NMD). One common characteristic of NMD, worthy of special mention, is skeletal muscle weakness and fatigue. This disorder affects the ability of the new exerciser to control the lifting of light weights. It is important that these individuals are closely supervised and that a spotter is available to render assistance. As far as the actual number of sets and repetitions are concerned, physically disabled individuals should be treated in the same manner as nondisabled persons. Consideration must be given to their previous experiences, medical history, and training goals.

Unlike the majority of physical disabilities, it is difficult for a fitness facility to cater to individuals with mental disabilities. First, most facilities do not have appropriately qualified personnel to deal with potential problems, and second, most businesses cannot afford to provide supervision. The foremost concern with mentally disabled individuals is safety. They require intense supervision, and consideration must be given to the layout of equipment and proximity to other users. Generally, exercises should be restricted to machines for safety purposes.

Weight Training and Injury Rehabilitation

Weight training has long been used in the rehabilitation of injuries, but recently the role of a fitness specialist also has been incorporated in the rehabilitation process. More patients are being referred to a gymnasium at an early stage in their recuperation, which requires fitness professionals to be knowledgeable about the recovery process. A fitness instructor now can design and administer a program with a patient under the guidance of a doctor, therapist, or athletic trainer.

After initial immobilization and healing of an injury, the aim is to gradually increase the connective tissue density and the strength of the muscle through the application of a stressor such as weights. Muscular strength is one of the essential factors in restoring the function of the body part to preinjury status. Three major types of muscular contraction are used in the rehabilitation process. An *isometric* exercise (a muscular contraction where the length of the muscle remains unchanged) can be used to increase the static strength of the muscle and assist in the reduction of muscle wastage. *Isotonic* contractions (performed by keeping a constant muscular force throughout the contraction) are beneficial because they provide a means for progressive exercise increases and are performed through a full range of motion. An *isokinetic* contraction (performed at a constant speed) can be used in the rehabilitation process because it enables a maximum load to be applied safely throughout the entire range of motion. In addition, the contraction speed can be predetermined, allowing total control of the movement.

The majority of equipment found in the gymnasium is suitable for injury rehabilitation. Weight machines generally can be adjusted to limit the range of movement, and some simulate a breaking system similar to that provided by expensive isokinetic machines (frequently used in therapy by athletic trainers). Free weights are especially useful in the latter stages of healing. The basic principle of rehabilitation is that of progressive resistance, whereby the treatment process begins with light loads that become progressively heavy with time.

Summary

The purpose of this section was to dispel some of the misconceptions that surround weight training with prepubescent children, pregnant women, elderly persons, and disabled individuals. Some of the issues that should be considered when designing a program for these groups are presented. One theme that is common to all groups is the importance of creating a safe environment for the exerciser and those working out in close proximity.

Glossary

abduction movement away from the body

absolute strength the maximal amount of force a muscle is able to sustain

acromegaly debilitating disorder that causes bones to thicken, in turn broadening the hands, face, and feet. Also causes a thickening of the skin and soft tissue growth

active stretch requires the person stretching to actively supply the force

actin fine protein thread of the muscle that is important for muscular contraction

adduction movement toward the body

adenosine triphosphate (ATP) energy-rich compound that provides the energy used by the body

aerobic in the presence of oxygen

agonist muscles that are primarily responsible for movement

amino acids building blocks for skeletal muscle

ampheramines substances that work to increase the stimulation of the central nervous system

anabolic steroids hormones that are similar to male sex hormones. The anabolic or building properties of these hormones increase the growth of muscle and bone tissue

anaerobic without oxygen

antagonist muscles that oppose the movement of the agonists

anxiety unpleasant emotional reaction that accompanies arousal

arousal physical reaction of the body and mental activation that represents the intensity level of behavior

auxiliary exercises move only a single joint and few muscle groups

ballistic stretching active stretching technique that requires the exerciser to produce a bouncing motion

barbells bars of varying length that hold weights at either end

blood doping increasing an individual's total volume of red blood cells

body composition amount of fat and nonfat components that make up the body

body-part exercise attempts to isolate one specific muscle or muscle group

bone mineral density amount of mineral deposited in a given area of bone

bone strength amount of force that bones are able to withstand

cardiac muscle muscle that is associated with the heart

cardiovascular endurance ability of the lungs, heart, and blood vessels to deliver oxygen to the body during prolonged physical activity

chalk powder or block form of calcium carbonate that improves the grip by absorbing perspiration

chromium trace element used in the regulation of glucose that has also been claimed to enhance performance

circumduction circular motion combining flexion, abduction, extension, and adduction

concentration narrowing and sharpening mental focus to maximize physical movements

concentric contraction in which the muscle shortens

core exercises require several body joints and muscles to move during the lift

creatine phosphate (CP) chemical important in the resynthesis of ATP

delayed-onset muscle soreness (DOMS) muscular pain caused by damaged muscle fibers that follows intense exercise

developmental stretch assists in increasing muscle and joint flexibility

dislocation injury in which the bones are separated at a joint

dumbbells handheld weights that can be used singularly or in a pair

duration amount of time spent on an exercise or workout

dynamic stretching amount of time spent on an exercise or workout

eccentric contraction in which the muscle exerts force as it lengthens

endomysium outermost structure of the muscle

ergogenic aids substances or phenomena that improve an individual's performance

extension increasing the angle of a joint in a straightening movement

fasciculi bundles of muscle fibers

flexibility possible range of movement of a joint and the surrounding muscle structures

flexion decreasing the angle of a joint in a folding or bending movement

free weights dumbbells, barbells, and weighted plates used in weight training

frequency number of times an exercise or workout is performed

general warm-up component transition from rest to light exercise, consisting of any exercise that involves movement of large muscle groups

genetics relates to causal antecedents, such as one's parents

glucose sugar stored in the body that releases energy used to form ATP

glycogen storage form of glucose

goal desired outcome to which the effort is directed

hormonal agents naturally occurring hormones believed to benefit the performance of physical activities

human growth hormone (hGH) naturally occurring hormone that aids in building muscle

hypertrophy increase in muscle mass caused by increasing the size and number of muscle cells

hypothermia dangerously low body temperature

intensity amount of weight that is being used

isokinetic contraction performed at a constant speed

isometric muscular contraction during which the length of the muscle remains unchanged

isotonic contraction performed by maintaining a constant force

lactic acid chemical formed during the breakdown of glucose to ATP when oxygen is not present

lifting straps canvas or leather straps that assist a lifter in maintaining a proper grip and control of the bar

load amount of weight lifted per repetition

macrocycle overall training period in a periodization model

mental rehearsal visualization technique used by an individual to practice a routine or action mentally, prior to performing

mesocycle one of several stages of training which make up a macrocycle

metabolism rate at which the body uses energy

microcycle periods of 1 week of training which are part of a mesocycle

mitochondria structures in the cell where ATP is produced for energy

muscle tone muscle tissue which is firm, sound, and flexible

muscular endurance ability of muscles to persist in exerting a force over a period of time

muscular power muscle's ability to release an explosive muscular force

muscular strength amount of force a muscle can exert against a resistance in one maximal effort

myofibrils make up the muscle fiber and are the site of muscular contraction

myosin fine protein thread of the muscle that is important for muscular contraction

nutrients compounds used by the body to provide energy and to aid in growth and repair

nutritional supplements nutrient that claims to possess bodybuilding or fat-burning properties

optimal zone of functioning zone where maximal results are achieved with a minimal amount of stress and strain

osteoporosis loss in bone mineral density and subsequent weakening of bone

periodization model of training that organizes sessions into cycles that differ in objectives, tasks, and content

pestle type of stone used by the Greeks in weight training that resembles the modern day dumbbell

pharmacological agents naturally occurring agents that are added in excess to the body in an attempt to increase its function in physical activity

phosphagens storage form of ATP and creatine phosphate

physiological agents substances that are naturally produced by the body and are used in excess in an attempt to increase physical activity

proteins complex molecules that are responsible for body growth, maintenance and repair, and energy production

psychology science of behavior and mental processes

repetition maximum (RM) load that can be lifted a given number of times

repetitions number of times an exercise movement is repeated consecutively

rest recovery time between sets of exercises and between sessions

rotation a pivoting movement of the bone on its own axis

set group of repetitions performed in one attempt of the same exercise

skeletal muscle muscles that are responsible for the movements of the body and support of the skeletal system

sliding filament theory common theory associated with muscular contraction

smooth muscle muscle associated with the internal organs that is able to contract without conscious effort

split workouts weight training program that emphasizes different muscle groups on different days of training

spotting assisting a person who is unable to safely accomplish an exercise

state anxiety feelings of apprehension and tension that vary from moment to moment

stress whole process by which we appraise and respond to events that threaten or challenge us

structural exercise requires the use of a number of different muscles to perform the exercise

synergists muscles that aid the agonists in performing movement

total-body workouts weight training program in which the lifter trains all the major muscle groups in one day

trace elements naturally occurring elements that are needed by the body in small quantities

trait anxiety part of a person's personality that is more constant and stable than state anxiety

tropomyosin protein that inhibits muscular contraction

troponin protein that pulls away tropomyosin allows muscular contraction to occur

type I (slow-twitch fiber) muscle fiber that is able to produce a small amount of force over a long period of time, characterized by utilizing oxygen when contracting

type II (fast-twitch fiber) muscle fiber that is able to produce a large, rapid force

vanadium trace element that has been claimed to have ergogenic effects

visualization process of mentally planning, creating, evaluating, and solving problems

volume for one session the number of repetitions x sets x load

weight belts wide, thick leather belts that are used to stabilize and protect the lower back

weight lifting gloves soft leather gloves that cover the palm of the hand and are used to improve the grip during weight training

weight machines equipment that restricts movement to ensure correct technique and safety. Weights are stacked and the resistance is altered by moving a pin that supports the weights

wellness constant and deliberate effort to stay healthy and achieve the highest potential for well-being

Index